In His Father's Image

The Father and Son Relationship Between God and Jehovah

In His Father's Image

The Father and Son Relationship Between God and Jehovah

By
Clay McConkie, Ph.D.

CFI
Springville, Utah

ISBN: 1-55517-775-1
e. 1

Published by CFI
An Imprint of Cedar Fort Inc.
www.cedarfort.com

Distributed by:

CEDAR
FORT

Typeset by Natalie Roach
Cover design by Nicole Shaffer
Cover design © 2004 by Lyle Mortimer

Printed in the United States of America
10 9 8 7 6 5 4 3 2 1
Printed on acid-free paper

Library of Congress Number: 2004114717

JEHOVAH

"For unto which of the angels said he at any time, Thou art my Son, this day have I begotten thee?

"And again, I will be to him a Father, and he shall be to me a Son?

"And again, when he bringeth in the first begotten into the world, he saith, And let all the angels of God worship him."

Hebrews 1:5-6

Table of Contents

1

A PRIMORDIAL BEGINNING

It is true that mankind, in one sense, has always existed, without any beginning or end. There was never a time, in other words, when the original substance making up body and spirit did not exist somewhere in the universe.

And yet there was definitely a time far back in the past when the primeval substance, by whatever method and circumstance, was organized into a body and came into existence, a body of spirit at first and later one of flesh and bones.

Before any of this happened, however, there was still a more distant time period, one about which little is known but where many significant things took place. It was a time when early forms of life that would eventually become human progressed and developed, as well as one where a specific relationship was established between the God of the Universe and the one who someday would become Jehovah. Indeed, it was during this primeval era that the concept and principle of the Father and the Son had its beginning.

Again there is only brief information about such an early existence, the time before anyone came into the world as spirit offspring of God or human beings.

Scriptural evidence, in fact, is almost non-existent. Yet there is enough to give a considerable amount of knowledge along with valuable clues and implications.

"Man was also in the beginning with God," the scripture says. "Intelligence, or the light of truth, was not created or made, neither indeed can be."

Certainly the word "intelligence" would normally suggest intellect and mental ability, but in this particular scripture it means much more than that. Rather than anything pertaining to learning and understanding, the word refers instead to a substance or form of matter, something that cannot be created or made but potentially is independent and self-existent. The same can be said for the word "truth" which also has an additional meaning.

"All truth is independent in that sphere in which God has placed it, to act for itself, as all intelligence also; otherwise there is no existence."[1]

Truth and intelligence, and particularly the latter, both refer to a spirit element or substance that has extraordinary capabilities. When the substance becomes self-existent, or in other words independent, it is able to do a variety of things, the most important of which is "to act for itself."

In the beginning, therefore, man existed in the presence of God. He did not as yet have a spirit body, but in his intelligence state he eventually did acquire the ability to act independently. This in turn implies decision making and the exercise of agency.

"Behold, here is the agency of man," states the scripture, "and here is the condemnation of man; because that which was from the beginning is plainly manifest unto them, and they receive not the light. And every man whose spirit receiveth not the light is under condemnation." 2

Man did not have to wait for a spirit body in order to think and exercise agency. Neither did he have to wait in order to progress or retrogress, as the circumstances might have been. As it would be in the future, he could now make decisions according to the light and knowledge given him. In the intelligence state, there was an opportunity to succeed and to prepare for what lay ahead. Each identity was in charge of its own destiny.

Although it is unknown to what extent man was actually a conscious identity at this point of progression, an entity that was aware of an individual personality, the scripture does say that God placed him in a sphere where he could act for himself, responding either positively or negatively to light and knowledge. It was definitely an opportunity for him to act or to be acted upon at this particular time, and not just one reserved for the future.

Unfortunately, from the beginning there were those who misused their agency at times and did not accept or receive the light. Yet there were many others who did. The most notable among these, of course, was Jehovah!

Down through the ages of time, God was well aware of what was taking place among those who were in a spirit state and regarded as intelligence. Well did he know when someone had advanced to a point where he could be given special consideration and be conformed to the image of his Son. Among the billions coming up through the ranks, so to speak, there were many who were competent and worthy, but only one that was eventually to be selected. He would be the first to enter the new world of spirits as a spirit being, the one who later would be known as Jehovah and who together with God himself would be the Father and the Son!

"For whom he did foreknow," the scripture says, "he also did predestinate (foreordain) to be conformed to the image of his Son, that he might be the firstborn among many brethren." 3

Undoubtedly there was a multitude of "brethren" who had qualified for the opportunity of joining Jehovah in becoming the first begotten spirits of the Father. He was the first, but others were close behind. People with the potential of Peter and John the Baptist, as well as outstanding women such as the Virgin Mary, might certainly be considered as being in this group. A list of such individuals, including prophets and patriarchs, would necessarily be very long.

But the important thing is that the process had begun. A new phase of existence and progression was now in operation. Finally, after ages of trial and testing, identities of intelligence that had long waited for a spirit body were now making the transition to a new world. The foremost among them was the Firstborn, but following him came a host of others who were also foreordained and called to be the first begotten sons and daughters of the Father!

2

THE GIFT OF AGENCY

There is no scriptural evidence that any kind of primordial spirit substance existed in the beginning except truth and intelligence, the material which eventually became self-existent and capable of "acting for itself." It is obvious, however, that before God placed this substance in a sphere where it was independent, it was nevertheless present in a dormant and rudimentary condition.

This suggests that intelligence at a very early stage is latent and inactive, waiting to be relocated to a designated place where it is given independence and knowledge, in addition to the ability to exercise agency.

"All truth is independent in that sphere in which God has placed it, to act for itself, as all intelligence also; otherwise there is no existence." [4]

Again there is the implication of a time period in which intelligence existed without independence and thinking ability. It was only after being placed in a different sphere that it acquired additional qualities necessary for further progression.

Yet whatever it was that actually happened, as well as when, the significant thing is that there was a specific time when the spirit substance was endowed with the power of agency, the ability to think for itself and choose between right and wrong.

For the first time, spirit element functioned in a new environment, each individual identity being in a sphere of activity where it was independent. If it were otherwise, according to the scripture, there would be no existence. The intelligence itself would still exist, since it was not created or made, but there would be no existence that involved thinking and reacting, as well as the use of agency.

It was highly significant, therefore, when man acquired his agency and the right to choose. Several important principles were necessarily involved. At least four things are said to be in operation in order for such a thing to take place, all of them being characteristic of the new environment in which God placed the newly-formed entities of spirit matter.

First, there needed to be some kind of law or commandment identifying what one should or should not do. Second, it was necessary to have a knowledge of good and evil. In the Garden of Eden, Adam and Eve obtained this knowledge by partaking of the forbidden fruit, but in an earlier setting those in the intelligence state would necessarily have had to receive it in a different way.

Third, there would need to be opposition, opposing forces pulling in the direction of either right or wrong. Fourth, permission and ability to choose must then be given to each individual identity, either to act or be acted upon in deciding which way to go.

All of this in turn gives new meaning and dimension to the term existence. As stated in scripture, existence for those in the intelligence state commenced at that point where man received his agency and made the transfer from spirit element to an individual identity. Prior to that event there was no meaningful existence.

It was also at this time that man became an agent unto himself with ability to act or to be acted upon. The knowledge of good and evil which he received gave him new freedom to choose the way that would eventually lead to eternal life in heaven or to a lower type of glory.

"Ye are free," say the scriptures, regarding those who obtain agency. "Ye are permitted to act for yourselves; for behold, God hath given you a knowledge and he hath made you free."[5] Indeed, people in this category became "free forever, knowing good from evil; to act for themselves and not to be acted upon."[6]

When Adam and Eve partook of the forbidden fruit, they placed themselves "in a state to act," or "in a state to act according to their wills and pleasures, whether to do evil or to do good."[7] But in primeval times it was God himself who placed man in this state or sphere, a condition in which for the first time he could benefit from knowledge and act for himself.

In this connection, however, there is again a question as to whether or not someone at this particular time was actually a conscious identity, and if so to what extent? Was he aware that he was an individual, for example, one capable not only of thinking and decision making, but an identity who was conscious of self and who possessed a certain range of emotions?

Obviously it would be easy to ascribe too much character and personality to man at this stage of development. And yet if it is true that he now had agency and the ability to choose between good and evil, between right and wrong, it would not be illogical to assume that he possessed not only intellect but also emotions.

Inherent in the attribute of agency there will always be the potential for error. Identities of spirit element, like human beings later on, would be susceptible to making mistakes. Indeed, there would be those who would fail to one degree or another and not live up to expectations.

"Behold, here is the agency of man, and here is the condemnation of man; because that which was from the beginning is plainly manifest unto them, and they receive not the light. And every man whose spirit receiveth not the light is under condemnation." [8]

Along with those who were less obedient, however, there were also the ones who more successfully received light and knowledge, progressing in many different areas of activity. According to intellect and emotional maturity, as well as obedience and spirituality, all who were in the sphere where God had placed them spread out in a wide spectrum of ability and achievement. Billions of identities moved forward in an eternal progression. And at the very front, when it came time to move into the next sphere of existence, ahead of everyone else was one individual, the one who came to be known as Jehovah.

The fact that this one identity progressed to the capability and spirituality which entitled him to be conformed to the image of the Son of God is a strong implication that he himself was a conscious identity, as were others in the intelligence state. He was the prime example of what man was capable of achieving and becoming in a new environment. The presence of knowledge, freedom, and agency, along with Jehovah's tremendous accomplishment, are all indicative not only of a sophisticated existence but one where man could develop to a very high level. It was also the place where he might have anticipated that someday he would obtain a spirit body, just as spirits in another time period far in the future would look forward to mortality and a body of flesh and bones.

But for the present, the focus was now on Jehovah, the individual and identity who had been foreordained and called to be the Son of God. As the first to enter a new phase of existence, he would one day occupy a throne at the right hand of God himself. From the very beginning as a spirit being, he would now be known forever as the first person to enter heaven, even the Firstborn, the first begotten spirit of the Father!

3

GOD THE FATHER

The scriptures say nothing about the early existence and lifetime of God the Father. Yet there is significant evidence that he did exist in the distant past, first as an entity of intelligence and later as a human being living upon an earth.

As in the case of Jehovah, the Father in a primeval time period went through certain basic processes, progressing from rudimentary intelligence to a sphere of existence where he acquired agency. Next he entered a first estate and received a spirit body and then later advanced into the second estate of mortality. He went through all of the stages as the Son, in other words, including eventual death and resurrection.

Evidence for this, although not in scripture, is found in the teachings of latter-day prophets. Joseph Smith and Lorenzo Snow, former presidents of the Church of Jesus Christ of Latter-day Saints, both referred to this doctrine: *"As man now is, God once was; As God now is, man may be."* [9]

In a confidential interview prior to Joseph's death, Lorenzo told him how he had come to believe in this principle. The response which he received from the Prophet was, "Brother Snow, that is true gospel doctrine, and it is a revelation from God to you." [10]

During a general conference of the Church, less than three months before Joseph Smith's martyrdom, he also made the following statements: "God himself was once as we are now, and is an exalted man, and sits enthroned in yonder heavens! That is the great secret."

"If the veil were rent today," Joseph said, "and the great God who holds this world in its orbit, and who upholds all worlds and all things by his power, was to make himself visible, I say if you were to see him today, you would see him like a man in form, like yourselves in all the person, image and very form as a man; for Adam was created in the very fashion, image, and like-ness of God, and received instructions from, and walked, talked, and conversed with him, as one man talks and communes with another."

"It is the first principle of the gospel to know for a certainty the character of God," he continued, "and to know that we may converse with him as one man con-verses with another, and that he was once a man; yea, that God himself, the Father of us all, dwelt on an earth, the same as Jesus Christ himself did." [11]

Obviously these were controversial ideas, and most people did not believe them at the time, but Joseph Smith and Lorenzo Snow both did, and they testified that they were true. And throughout his long lifetime, this belief for Lorenzo was a constant light and guide.

"It was a bright, illuminating star before him all the time," his son later recalled, "in his heart, in his soul, and all through him." [12]

While people in the world continue to believe in a multitude of philosophies and doctrines, this one principle concerning God the Father is the one beyond all others that is important. It is the concept upon which all other principles necessarily exist. Certainly it is a paradox that such a panorama of eternity, so called, can be reduced to one small couplet!

> *"As man now is,*
> *God once was;*
> *As God now is*
> *Man may be."*[13]

Such a belief, of course, is not readily received by people in general. Yet is a belief and theory of evolution that allegedly someday will be acknowledged by everyone as being accurate and true. It is one also that is accompanied by an increased knowledge of God himself, telling where he is at present and who he really is.

The Father, for example, is said to be at a specific location in the universe or galaxy and is in charge over all things. His residence, according to modern scripture, is on a large orb or planet, surrounded by other planets called "the governing ones." In a revelation given to the patriarch Abraham, the Lord referred to the most important of these other planets as Kolob, it being the greatest among them because it is "nearest unto the throne of God."

"These are the governing ones," He told Abraham, "and the name of the great one is Kolob, because it is near unto me, for I am the Lord thy God: I have set this one to govern all those which belong to the same order as that upon which thou standest."

Abraham then continued with the account: "And

the Lord said unto me, by the Urim and Thummim, that Kolob was after the manner of the Lord, according to its times and seasons in the revolutions thereof; that one revolution was a day unto the Lord after his manner of reckoning, it being one thousand years according to the time appointed unto that whereon thou standest. This is the reckoning of the Lord's time, according to the reckoning of Kolob."[14]

The planet Kolob, therefore, is distinctive because it is the one closest to the place where God lives! Certainly out of the vast accumulation of scientific facts and astronomic details, this remarkable piece of information has to be one of the most significant statements that could possibly be made.

At the same time, it is the kind of statement that naturally invites criticism and difference of opinion. Some will say, for example, that it is presumptuous even to suggest that God is a being with an individual personality and a body of flesh and bones, much less saying that he resides on a specific planet in the universe! Yet it is true according to modern scripture, and Joseph Smith and Lorenzo Snow would both agree.

These two men, once again, were the first proponents of the belief that God once lived on an ordinary planet, working out his own personal salvation. In addition, they said that he is presently a glorified personage, a resurrected being who has reached the zenith of knowledge and accomplishment which entitles him to be the supreme power in the galaxy or universe.

And yet in the complete matrix of things and in an overall context, also according to an accurate theory of evolution, God himself had a father. There was a certain time period, in other words, far back in the past, when God was not only begotten by his own set of parents in heaven, but also by mortal parents at a later time on an earth. Again it was a case of him going through all of the basic processes that his Son would go through later on, from the early stages of intelligence to death and resurrection, and finally to Godhood.

It was in this last position where he would then preview those who were still in an intelligence state, choosing one of them to be foreordained and conformed to the image of his Son. Surely this was Jehovah, the first to enter the new world of spirits in premortality and the one also who was the Firstborn of the Father.

4

JEHOVAH: THE FIRSTBORN

When Jehovah acquired a body and entered the world as a spirit being, there were others who came with him. These undoubtedly included individuals who had been extremely successful in receiving light and knowledge and exercising agency, as well as having excelled in spirituality.

As to who these people might have been, it would not be surprising if Abraham and Moses were both among them, along with the unnamed spirit who eventually became the Holy Ghost. Based upon obedience and past performance, there would probably be a vast array of qualified individuals, all who had achieved a high standing in the intelligence state and who could now be considered, in a secondary way, also as first-born.

"For whom he did foreknow," the scripture says, referring to the Father and his knowledge of Jehovah as an intelligence, "he also did predestinate (foreordain) to be conformed to the image of his Son, that he might be the firstborn among many brethren."[15]

Reference to "many brethren" theoretically could mean all of those who followed after Jehovah, the billions who later made up the human race and family, yet a much more exclusive group is definitely implied. Among the latter would be the very elite of those who had been intelligence, including people such as the biblical patriarchs and prophets.

But still it was Jehovah, the first and most outstanding among all spirit beings, who was the supreme achiever and exemplar. Not enough can be said of him at this point of existence. His achievement prior to spirit birth was phenomenal, with or without being a conscious identity, and his potential must have been godlike almost from the beginning.

His standing as firstborn, of course, in and of itself gave him a marked superiority. This particular title, publicized in biblical history during the days of Jacob, or Israel, and also in the time of Moses, referred to certain rights and privileges given to the firstborn son of a father. Because of the timing of the son's birth, it signified that he was entitled to significant power and authority, at the same time acquiring additional responsibility. In ancient times, for example, the firstborn son, according to the principle of primogeniture, received a double portion of an inheritance but was also responsible for the care and protection of other family members.

Yet the important thing was that the firstborn was to represent his father and carry out his will, both while the father was alive and also after his death. In a sense, he was not only the oldest son, but the head of the family as well.

Unfortunately, there were times when the firstborn did not succeed in these duties. Jacob's brother Esau was one of these. The brothers were the twin sons of Isaac and Rebecca, and although Esau was the first to be born and consequently had the birthright, he did not value it, choosing instead to relinquish it to Jacob. Years later, Jacob's oldest son Reuben essentially did the same thing. Disregarding his responsibility to both father and family, he forfeited his birthright when he broke an important law of chastity.

In actuality, therefore, the principle of birthright and primogeniture was sometimes a very transient thing. Especially in the House of Israel, the famous organization named after Jacob, the birthright changed in a very short time from one person's hands to another.

From Reuben it passed to the next-to-the-youngest son Joseph, and from there jointly to Joseph' two sons, Manasseh the elder and his younger brother Ephraim. Then sometime later, and for whatever reason, it ended up in the sole possession of Ephraim, all of which showed that the function of birthright was not only transient but also unpredictable.

In the grand precedent set by Jehovah, of course, the idea was that during mortality, the position or office of firstborn was to be a reflection of integrity and responsibility, residing with the first male child born into a family. This person would then become a leader and example to those who followed, establishing a significant genealogical chain system down through time. And although it is not generally known how the system operated and fared anciently, it was obviously, among other things, a principle designed to foster family unity and stability.

In regard to the person of Jehovah, however, it was definitely a mark of achievement and seniority. He was the premier being among those in the intelligence state who had reached the highest level of success. Out of the countless number of entities that had been organized from spirit matter and placed in a sphere where they could act for themselves, he was the one who had excelled. He was the one individual that the Father eventually foreordained and conformed to the image of his Son.

"I will make him my firstborn," God said, "higher than the kings of the earth. My mercy will I keep for him for evermore, and my covenant shall stand fast for him."[16]

To those who revered Jehovah, he was "the image of the invisible God, the firstborn of every creature." [17] He was "the faithful and true witness, the beginning of the creation of God." [18]

On one occasion, as recorded in modern scripture, it was Jehovah himself who said, "I was in the beginning with the Father, and am the Firstborn; and all those who are begotten through me are partakers of the glory of the same, and are the church of the Firstborn." [19]

Again it was Jehovah who had advanced so remarkably down through the ages and had earned the right to be the first one born into the new world of spirits. He was the first individual to leave an early existence and begin a first estate. By doing so he became the potential head of a future church bearing his name, one that would originate during his brief stay in mortality and then many centuries later be reintroduced and restored in the latter days. Indeed, this was the Church of the Firstborn and would continue to exist throughout the eternities!

5

A NEW WORLD

Implicit in the doctrine that God once lived on an earth as a mortal being is the idea that he also had a wife. Much later as an exalted couple in heaven, the two were partners in bringing forth spirit offspring from among those who were in the final stages of intelligence. By way of a type of procreation, they begat spirit children after their likeness and image, male and female, and consequently a huge multitude of men and women began coming into a new world.

Stated in such a way, succinctly and matter-of-factly, this type of description is not apt to invite widespread acceptance, but in essence it is exactly what happened. Instead of the human race evolving in any other way, it was simply a matter of people becoming the offspring of divine parentage, [20] "begotten sons and daughters unto God." [21]

Accepting the concept of a mother in heaven, therefore, in addition to a father, is inescapable, albeit it be an unorthodox way of thinking. But if it is true that "God once was, as man now is," living on an earth and going through the same basic processes of existence, a marital relationship in regard to God the Father has to be included. Men like Joseph Smith and Lorenzo Snow would both subscribe to such an idea, although once again there is no scriptural evidence.

The same is true with another important concept, one pertaining to the new world of spirits and the subject of gender. Whether or not there were male and female identities prior to spirit birth, for example, is unknown, although it is a possibility. It might be that only tendencies toward one gender or the other developed in the intelligence state, but since agency was involved, it could also be that the new identities, to some degree, might have had a choice. Otherwise, the decision would be up to Deity at the time of birth.

A much more crucial decision, however, as well as a final judgment, was concerning which forms of life would be human and which would necessarily be otherwise. Which identities of intelligence, in other words, had prepared themselves to be human beings, and which had qualified only to enter lower levels of existence?

Just as people far in the future would be judged according to their works and assigned to a final kingdom of glory, so it is logical that the primordial identities of intelligence at one time or another also were judged and categorized, being assigned to their own kingdoms, as it were, whether to be humans, beasts, fish, birds, or insects. Through a process similar to natural selection and the survival of the fittest, identities ended up at a particular level, depending on how well they had adjusted to their environment and how successful they had been in adapting to the sphere in which God had placed them.

But whatever it was that happened, those coming into the new world of spirits who had human potential now began a new process of selection, individuals again being tested to see how they would react, and to what extent they could survive under new conditions and circumstances. In what later came to be known as the first estate, God determined especially to see how obedient people were. For the first time, beings possessed a spirit body and additional consciousness, each being aware that he or she was a spirit child of God and was finally on the way to future immortality and an opportunity for eternal life.

Certainly it was a time of continuing growth, building on whatever status had been acquired during the state of intelligence. With a spirit body, individuals could now progress with increased awareness and ability, emotionally and intellectually as well as spiritually. Everyone possessed a new identity.

As a consequence, people in varying degrees became educated in many different areas of knowledge, including the arts and sciences and also religion. They acquired individual features of personality along with important skills and aptitudes. Again it was a brand new world and a very formative period.

And among all of the knowledge and personal traits which people obtained, the most important by far, from Deity's point of view, was undoubtedly spirituality. The main reason for a first estate, to begin with, was to provide the type of education that would adequately prepare one for a challenging future which lay ahead.

"We will go down, for there is space there," God said, in preparing for an earth experience, "and we will take of these materials, and we will make an earth whereon these may dwell, and we will prove them herewith, to see if they will do all things whatsoever the Lord their God shall command them; and they who keep their first estate shall be added upon; and they who keep not their first estate shall not have glory in the same kingdom with those who keep their first estate." [22]

The religious aspect of things, therefore, was to be especially important in dealing with the inevitable challenges of the future. There would be conflicting philosophies and viewpoints, for example, requiring people to make vital decisions. Agency was still the right of every individual, but decisions would often be difficult, and the day was rapidly approaching when a severe crisis would develop in heaven itself and a critical choice would have to be made, certainly a very personal one with eternal consequences.

And when such an event finally did occur, a most unfortunate time in the Kingdom of Heaven, a large segment of people succumbed to a radical concept and ideology, an idea contrary not only to the majority of public opinion but to the will of God as well. It was a time when a third part of the hosts of heaven lost all rights and privileges and was permanently cast out! Even the suggestion of such a thing had never occurred, and when it did happen, it was an extremely tragic event.

The problem first arose during a council meeting sometime after the creation of the earth. The main subject was who would be the redeemer of mankind during a future mortality. There would necessarily come a time when an atonement would need to be made for personal sins committed by the people, and someone had to be chosen who could perform it, someone who would be an advocate and mediator representing the Father.

Of course the logical person to do this was Jehovah, the Firstborn and God's choice from the beginning, but another came forward and proposed that he also should be considered. This was Lucifer, referred to as "a son of the morning" and an individual who had acquired considerable authority in heaven.

A final question before the council was which of two concepts or ideologies should be selected, one introduced by Lucifer where an atonement would guarantee eventual salvation and exaltation to everyone, or one endorsed by both God and Jehovah where such an award would be conditional, dependent upon individual works and accomplishment. Apparently there was heavy representation and support on both sides, inside the council and without, and when all of the discussion and debate had taken place, the time arrived for a decision.

"And the Lord said: Whom shall I send? And one answered like unto the Son of Man: Here am I, send me. And another answered and said: Here am I, send me. And the Lord said: I will send the first. And the second was angry and kept not his first estate; and at that day, many followed after him." 23

In opposition to Lucifer, referred to scripturally as the red dragon, was a man whose name was Michael, someone who had also achieved considerable notability in heaven. It was he who now championed Jehovah's cause and became the commander in chief against Lucifer's forces.

"And there was war in heaven," states the scripture. "Michael and his angels fought against the dragon; and the dragon fought and his angels, and prevailed not;

neither was their place found anymore in heaven." The red dragon was defeated, therefore, "and his tail drew the third part of the stars of heaven and did cast them to the earth." 24

Again it was a time of tragedy almost beyond comprehension. In terms of eternal progression and the number of lives involved, it was an event unparalleled and unprecedented. After eons of preparation in the sphere of intelligence, a tremendous multitude of people, including Lucifer, were sentenced to permanent exile, to an unretractable expulsion from heaven!

Gone forever was the opportunity to live upon an earth and gain immortality. Even more tragic was the loss of an opportunity to gain exaltation and eternal life. Just as myriads of identities during intelligence had been denied a chance to receive a spirit body with human potential, being assigned instead to categories of beasts, fish, fouls, or insects, so now a third part of the hosts of heaven was denied a chance to continue an eternal progression, being cast out instead to an outer darkness. Their destiny there was to become companions and followers of Lucifer.

"And that great dragon was cast out, that old serpent called the Devil and Satan, which deceived the whole world: he was cast out to the earth, and his angels were cast out with him."25

As a consequence of what happened, it has since become well-known that one-third of heaven's population fell from grace and became lost spiritually. A third of all spirits forfeited whatever standing they might have had, along with any opportunity for further progression. An enormous throng of men and women began an eternal existence as so-called "sons of perdition!"

Yet in retrospect, it might be that things were actually not that bad. Thirty-three per cent of the population of heaven at the time, even allowing for the possibility that people were still coming in from the sphere of intelligence, could add up to an almost unbelievable number, suggesting that it might be unreasonable to think that God, on a single occasion, would lose such a huge percentage of people. It could be, in fact, that the calculated number involved has been exaggerated.

Demographers estimate that 69 to 110 billion people have been born on the earth since the time of Adam. If one-third of that preliminary amount alone is regarded as the number that rebelled during premortality, the significance of such a statistic is staggering, especially when the individuals involved are "the devil and his angels." The latter are not just spirit elements of influence, but thinking and rebellious people with spirit bodies!

Scriptural references to "the third part of the stars of heaven" or "a third part of the hosts of heaven," for example, might easily be interpreted as being one-third. But such an interpretation is not necessarily true. To the contrary, the term "third part" can be visualized as being something quite different.

Certainly another way of analyzing these scriptures is to think of three separate groups or parts, referring to large congregations of people, two parts being either similar or very different in size, but a third and much smaller part being the one that was eliminated. The third part definitely would not have to contain an exorbitant or alarming number.

And yet whatever it was that actually happened, the

tragedy of the event is still there, albeit it on a different scale. Again it is the idea that many identities had been successful in the past, progressing from a sphere of intelligence to the status of spirit beings, only to fail on the threshold of a new life and existence. An opportunity of inestimable proportions and magnitude was gone forever. A huge multitude and congregation of people, comprising an untold number of billions, forfeited the opportunity of going to earth, not as spirit angels of the Devil but as mortal men and women with bodies of flesh and bones, all under the direct supervision of God the Father and Jehovah!

6

PREPARATION FOR EARTH

Many important events took place in heaven in preparation for mortality and the beginning of a second estate. One of these was the creation of the earth. "In the beginning," the Bible says, "God created the heaven and the earth. And the earth was without form, and void. And darkness was upon the face of the deep." [26]

By this time it was Jehovah who was in charge of creation under his Father's direction. Jehovah, subsequent to the time that he had become the Firstborn, had now risen to the status of Godhood and had attained to the position where he was creator of not just one world but many.

"He was in the world," the Bible continues, referring to Jehovah "and the world was made by him, and the world knew him not."

"All things were made by him; and without him was not anything made that was made." [27]

Again the magnificence of this one individual is almost beyond comprehension and understanding. From the very beginning, even in the sphere of intelligence, there was something about his particular spirit and identity that was marked for a supreme destiny. His very existence implied an inherent tendency toward the Divine. In the primeval past the Father had known well who he was, and "whom he did foreknow, he also did predestinate (foreordain) to be conformed to the image of his Son." 28

Especially in modern scripture is there a statement about his subsequent glory and power: "That by him, and through him, and of him, the worlds are and were created, and the inhabitants thereof are the begotten sons and daughters unto God." 29

The process of creation, therefore, was the sole responsibility of Jehovah, always acting in behalf of the Father. One was conducting, in other words, and the other presided. At the same time there were additional people involved, one being Michael, who led the Lord's forces during the war against Lucifer in heaven. But among all those who participated, it was Jehovah who was preeminent.

"And then the Lord said: Let us go down. And they went down at the beginning, and they, that is the Gods, organized and formed the heavens and the earth."

"And they said: Let there be light; and there was light. And they commanded the light, for it was bright; and they divided the light, or caused it to be divided, from the darkness." 30

Thus through the instrumentality of Jehovah, and also Michael and others working with him, the planet earth was organized and formed, and in a sense created. Situated in an orbit revolving around the sun, where for a time it would exist among other bodies in a solar system, it was to be one of the key planets in the universe, the one where Jehovah would later be born as a mortal and would perform the infinite atonement for mankind. It was a shining jewel, so to speak, among the Lord's creations.

It was also the designated place, once again, where those who had been companions with the Lord as spirits, and earlier as intelligence, would soon be sent to earth for additional experience and testing. By way of a carefully executed program of planning and logistics, the machinery was established for introducing a gigantic number of people at the right time and in the right place. Specific individuals were selected in advance, according to the foreknowledge of God, to provide leadership and to fulfill important missions.

Jehovah himself was the first of these, having been foreordained in the beginning and conformed to the image of God's son, as well as being named the future Redeemer. Following him came the foreordination and calling of many others, all in preparation for an earth experience which lay ahead. "Moreover, whom he did predestinate (foreordain), them he also called, and whom he called, them he also justified, and whom he justified, them he also glorified." [31]

Among all of these people were undoubtedly Adam and the early patriarchs such as Enoch, Noah, and Melchizedek, and also the great prophet Abraham. In his own words, as recorded in modern scripture, the latter at one time referred to his own foreordination and calling: "Now the Lord had shown unto me, Abraham, the intelligences that were organized before the world was; and among all these were many of the noble and great ones; and God saw these souls that they were good, and he stood in the midst of them, and he said: These I will make my rulers; for he stood among those that were spirits, and he saw that they were good.

"And he said unto me: Abraham, thou art one of them; thou wast chosen before thou wast born." [32]

It was this particular prophet who would later initiate the famous genealogical lines referred to as the seed of Abraham, and more significantly people within those lines known as the children of promise. In addition, he would become the grandfather of Jacob, the man who had twelve sons and was the originator of the earthly organization known as the House of Israel.

Down through time, as the earth's history unfolded, God spoke with many prophets and patriarchs, giving them encouragement and instructions, but the important thing is that on these occasions, Jehovah was the one in charge, acting under the direction of his Father. Although it is not always apparent in scripture that it is he who is speaking, it is Jehovah nevertheless supervising world affairs and consequently the one regarded not only as the God of the Old Testament but also God of the world.

It was Jehovah, therefore, who directed operations for the future populating of the earth. He established the various lineages and designated the geographical areas where people would be located. According to a predetermined plan, he provided that some, because of their obedience and accomplishment, would receive preferential treatment, being placed in locations and under conditions which would be more to their advantage. As a consequence, they would have additional opportunity to be successful during their stay on earth.

The people in this particular group, in essence, were the Israelites in heaven, a separate and distinct segment of previous society. Although Jacob, also known as Israel, had not been born yet, and the House of Israel on earth had not yet been formed, still there were those in the new world of spirits who can definitely be viewed as an early version of the Israelite kingdom, a House of Israel in and of itself, as it were, and the group also used by Jehovah as a guide and reference as he populated the earth.

"Remember the days of old," the Bible states, "consider the years of many generations: ask thy father, and he will shew thee; thy elders, and they will tell thee. When the most High divided to the nations their inheritance, when he separated the sons of Adam, he set the bounds of the people according to the number of the children of Israel."

In paraphrase, it might be said that Jehovah established the lineages and set the bounds of the people according to whether or not they were members of the House of Israel. The Bible then continues by saying, "For the Lord's portion is his people; Jacob is the lot of his inheritance." 33

In the previous world before mortality, sometimes referred to as the preexistence, those who were more religious and obedient were regarded as the Lord's people, that portion of heaven that was more spiritual. In a significant way, they were the inheritance of both Jehovah and his Father, the group of people who later on earth would be called the descendants of Jacob or the children of Israel.

Is it a possibility also that this group was one of three parts of heaven during the time of Lucifer's rebellion? When he and his angels rebelled, in other words, did the

House of Israel along with another part remain faithful while a third part was cast out?

Whatever the answers to such questions might be, when it came time for the transfer of people from a first estate to mortality, a so-called Israelite connection apparently was a very important factor. Whether or not people were members of the House of Israel in heaven, for example, became very crucial in their deployment to a particular place and status on earth. Certainly it was the main guide and index in establishing the different lineages. And as men and women now completed their first estate in the world of spirits, they were ready to begin a very new kind of existence with a new type of body, one that was vitalized for the first time with the element of blood and also constructed of flesh and bones!

7

THE HOUSE OF ISRAEL

As an earthly organization, the House of Israel did not have a scriptural beginning until the time of Jacob. It began after he left his home in Palestine and went into Mesopotamia to escape a death threat from his brother Esau, in which place he married two of his cousins and started raising a family. Eventually he had two other wives, and upon leaving years later, his family consisted of eleven sons and a daughter. One other son was soon born, after which the House of Israel officially came into existence.

While returning home to Palestine, Jacob was twice informed that his name was being changed to Israel, first by an angel or messenger, and then by the Lord himself who undoubtedly was Jehovah. "And God said unto him, Thy name is Jacob: Thy name shall not be called anymore Jacob, but Israel shall be thy name: And he called his name Israel."34

In the years that followed, Jacob's sons began having families of their own, and at the time that they journeyed into Egypt with their father during a famine, the group numbered sixty-six people, not counting the sons' wives, and was referred to as the House of Jacob. Many years later, as Moses led their descendants out of Egyptian bondage toward the promised land, the posterity of Jacob had become a mighty people, the men alone being more than 600,000 in number according to the Bible. At that time they were known as the House of Israel.

In actuality, however, Israelites themselves had been a part of society much earlier. Righteous individuals born on earth, starting with the time of Adam, presumably came from that part of heaven's population which had been the most obedient and spiritual. These were the so-called "children of Israel" in premortality. Consequently, because of the type of life which they had led during their first estate, they were now entitled to more optimum circumstances and living conditions on earth. It was to their advantage to be born within the patriarchal line of Adam and his immediate successors.

The unusual group of people during the days of Enoch, those who were translated together as a city into heaven, most likely were Israelites before birth, later being located advantageously and eventually attaining to a high level of spirituality. Others associated with the patriarchal line would be in a similar category. But unfortunately such a condition was not widespread, since by the time of Noah people had generally become so corrupted that they were subject to annihilation. An implication in their case would be that the flow of Israelites from heaven had temporarily been interrupted.

Visualizing a favored Israelite population coming from premortality, therefore, is not without complication. The idea that people were more apt to be successful during a tenure on earth after having been treated preferentially was apparently not always true, either that or such people were not of Israelite origin to begin with.

It is logical, nevertheless, to say that long before the time of Jacob, as far back as Adam and Eve, people were living upon the earth who definitely had been part of a separate and distinct group in the premortal world, those who might be regarded as Israelites in the beginning and who later were comparable to descendants of Jacob and the children of Israel. They were among the people who, as a reward for righteous living, had been born at a favored time and place on earth, occasions when God "determined the times before appointed, and the bounds of their habitation." [35]

Once again it was Jehovah who directed all of these activities and was in charge of operations. He was the "Most High," acting under the direction of his Father, who supervised the populating of the earth according to a preconceived plan from the time of Adam down to Abraham, Isaac, and Jacob, and from there to the time of Moses. He it was who administered the affairs pertaining to the people. "When the most High divided to the nations their inheritance," the scripture says, "when he separated the sons of Adam, he set the bounds of the people according to the number of the children of Israel." [36]

It is also significant in this regard, as noted in the Bible, that God allegedly spoke to ancient Israel in particular only as God Almighty and not as Jehovah.

"I appeared to Abraham, unto Isaac, and unto Jacob," he said, speaking to Moses, "by the name of God Almighty, but by my name JEHOVAH was I not known to them." [37]

And although the translation of this passage has been questioned, it is interesting that the name of

Jehovah is used at all, it being a definite rarity in biblical scripture. The verity and correct interpretation of the name, however, and the concept that it embraces, is well expressed in the Book of Psalms where it says that "men may know that thou, whose name alone is JEHOVAH, art the most high over all the earth." [38]

Certainly it was Jehovah who continued to guide the affairs of people all down through history, so notably during the lifetime of Moses and the historic exodus from Egypt. The introduction of the Ten Commandments and the accompanying principles and ordinances in this time period constitute an important part of religion in both the Old and New Testaments. And there is no doubt but what their authorship was that of Jehovah.

On one occasion, for example, concerning the Law of Moses, he said, "Behold, I am he that gave the law, and I am he who covenanted with my people Israel. Behold, I am the law, and the light. Look unto me, and endure to the end, and ye shall live; for unto him that endureth to the end will I give eternal life." [39]

Following the time of Moses and the succeeding period of Judges in Palestine, as well as during the reigns of Saul, David, and Solomon, the people known as Israelites increased in population and continued as a nation, generally retaining a common identity. Then in approximately 930 B.C. they divided into two separate groups, the Kingdom of Israel in the north and the Kingdom of Judah in the south. The northern kingdom, comprising the Ten Tribes, continued for a little over 200 years before being conquered by the Assyrians. The southern kingdom, which contained two tribes plus the priestly tribe of Levi, suffered a similar fate at the hands of the Chaldeans of Babylonia 135 years later.

As a consequence, the people known as the House of Israel were scattered, and in the future they would continue to be scattered into many different parts of the earth. Their condition became an important factor in evolving world history. It was particularly significant that some of those in the former Kingdom of Judah eventually reassembled in the area of Jerusalem in southern Palestine where they became the nucleus of a large Jewish population in the time of Jesus.

This latter time period, of course, is well known and documented in both biblical and modern scripture. It is unique that the Firstborn of the Father was no longer acting as Jehovah but in the person of Jesus, the Only Begotten. Especially while the latter was growing into manhood in Palestine, the administration of human affairs, which formerly had been Jehovah's responsibility, were temporarily assumed by the Father.

Immediately following the Lord's crucifixion and resurrection, however, it was obvious once again who was in command. In the Western Hemisphere, where thousands were killed in a series of earthquakes and natural disasters, it was definitely Jehovah who administered widespread destruction and retribution because of "iniquity and abominations" among the people. Referring to himself as he had been known in mortality, he spoke to all of those who had been spared.

"Behold, I am Jesus Christ the Son of God," he said on that occasion. "I created the heavens and the earth, and all things that in them are. I was with the Father from the beginning. I am in the Father, and the Father in me; and in me hath the Father glorified his name."

"O ye people in these great cities which have fallen, who are the descendants of Jacob, yea, who are of the house of Israel, how oft have I gathered you as a hen gathereth her chickens under her wings and have nourished you."

"O ye people of the house of Israel, ye that dwell at Jerusalem, as ye that have fallen; yea, how oft would I have gathered you as a hen gathereth her chickens, and ye would not."[40]

Surely it was a sad commentary at that time concerning the earth's population, and after the Lord's ascension into heaven, following the time of the early apostles, a tremendous void occurred in which there was a decrease in accounts telling of either Jehovah or His Father. Only in modern scripture, including material written by prophets living on the American continent, is there any mention of Deity's continued administration of affairs in heaven or those of the House of Israel.

Just as there were subsequent events such as the fall of the Roman Empire and the emergence of the Dark Ages, followed by eras of reformation and enlightenment, so also was there a long period during world history in which religious groups reported no new revelation or canonized scripture. There was a Dark Ages in religion itself, in other words, although one in which the presence of Jehovah was undoubtedly still an important factor. It is logical to assume that a certain number of people still continued to come from a premortal House of Israel. Such might have comprised any number of righteous people, including outstanding religious reformers such as John Calvin and Martin Luther.

But it was not until the latter days, during a period of history known as the Dispensation of the Fulness of Times, that a full-scale emigration of Israelites apparently began making the transition from a first to a second estate. God and Jehovah had reserved this particular time period as one that would be preparatory to the Second Coming of Jesus Christ, one also that would be the scene of a dramatic culmination of world events and circumstances, among which would be the gathering of scattered Israel and the restoration of those referred to as the Ten Tribes.

In a dispensation following six others, those led by Adam, Enoch, Noah, Abraham, and Moses, as well as Jesus Christ, a final period in history began to unfold and was presided over by someone with a very common name, a man known only as Joseph Smith. This latter-day individual, who by inference was one of the elite in premortality and a preeminent figure in the original House of Israel, was allegedly the one person who was instrumental in restoring to the earth all of the important truths that had been revealed in past dispensations.

It was predicted, in other words, that God would someday institute among the world's people a marvelous work and a wonder, revealing to them all wisdom and knowledge, "having made known unto us the mystery of his will, according to his good pleasure which he has purposed in himself: that in the dispensation of the fulness of times he might gather together in one all things in Christ, both which are in heaven, and which are on earth; even in him." [41]

It was also in this final time period, and very appropriately so, that an unprecedented event took place as the dispensation began. For the first time in human history and in the annals of the House of Israel, God the Father and his Son Jehovah appeared together and talked to a man on earth. He was a very young man at the time, born in humble circumstances and unschooled, but he was evidently the precise one that God had selected. The one designated once again was the man known as Joseph Smith

Not since the Garden of Eden had there been an occasion when the Father and the Son together had made such an appearance. And very significantly, as might be expected at this particular time, it was the Father who spoke first, but only briefly, and then turned the time over to Jehovah.

"This is my beloved Son," he said. "Hear him." [42]

This unusual visitation was in answer to a prayer in which Joseph Smith asked which of existing churches was correct, and which one he should join. The answer from Jehovah was that he should join none of them, but that in the future he would be the one to organize a new church, patterned after the original one which existed in the days of the early apostles. This was to be part of the restitution of all things spoken of in the Bible and would be accomplished through the manifestation of angels and by way of priesthood authority. Indeed, as things eventually turned out, this was also the commencement of a brand new era of history and the final dispensation of time!

8

JESUS AND THE LOST TRIBES

When the Kingdom of Israel and the ten tribes fell to the Assyrians in the latter part of the eighth century B.C., it was a devastating blow to the House of Israel. Thousands of people were uprooted from their homes in northern and central Palestine, as well as in nearby Transjordan, and deported to various sections of the Assyrian Empire. Thousands of others were left behind to mix with foreign colonists coming in from conquered areas.

More than a hundred years later, the Chaldeans led by Nebuchadnezzar invaded the Kingdom of Judah, completely destroying the capital city of Jerusalem and bringing the second kingdom to a close. Again much of the population was taken captive, this time to Babylonia, and the House of Israel was further fragmented and scattered. As predicted in prophecy, the people of Israel were sifted "among the nations, like as corn is sifted in a sieve." [43]

Many of the Judah captives eventually returned to Jerusalem to rebuild the city and temple, but there was a much different situation among some of those in the Kingdom of Israel who had been deported to Assyria. A certain number, for example, sometime between the sixth and seventh Centuries B.C., left their places of captivity and traveled further north, mysteriously disappearing and later becoming known as the lost tribes. These were people whom Jesus would later visit soon after his resurrection and ascension into heaven.

And yet prior to that event, and in this same time period, he would appear to still another group of people, those who had once been part of the Kingdom of Judah but had crossed the seas and were now living in the Western Hemisphere.

During his earthly ministry, Jesus said on one occasion that there were others besides those in Palestine that he needed to visit. "And other sheep I have," he said, "which are not of this fold: them also I must bring, and they shall hear my voice; and there shall be one fold and one shepherd."44 Those who heard him at that time thought he meant non-Jewish people in surrounding areas, but as it turned out, he was speaking of a much more distant group. And when he later visited these people in what is now possibly the vicinity of Central America, he told them that they were the ones he had referred to earlier.

"And verily I say unto you," he said, "that ye are they of whom I said: Other sheep I have which are not of this fold."

"Behold, ye have both heard my voice and seen me; and ye are my sheep, and ye are numbered among those whom the Father hath given me." 45

On this historic visit, soon after his ascension from Palestine, Jesus spent several days among the people known as the Nephites, teaching them and performing many signs and miracles. He also chose twelve men to be a select group of disciples. These twelve, comparable to the twelve apostles in Jerusalem, were set apart as special witnesses.

At this time he announced himself as Jesus Christ, it being only a few weeks after his death when he spoke out of darkness to the people in the Western Hemisphere who had been spared during widespread holocaust and destruction. In reality it was Jehovah who said, "And many great destructions have I caused to come upon this land, and upon this people, because of their wickedness and abominations." [46] But now following his resurrection, as he had done in Palestine, he appeared to the people as Jesus Christ, being announced to them by his Father.

It was also at this time that he told them there was still a third group that he would soon visit. "And verily, verily, I say unto you," he said, "that I have other sheep which are not of this land, neither of the land of Jerusalem, neither in any parts of that land round about whither I have been to minister. For they of whom I speak are they who have not as yet heard my voice; neither have I at any time manifested myself unto them.

"But I have received a commandment of the Father that I shall go unto them, and that they shall hear my voice, and shall be numbered among my sheep, that there may be one fold and one shepherd; therefore I go to show myself unto them." [47]

These were the lost tribes, therefore, that segment of people among those taken captive into Assyria from the Kingdom of Israel who eventually banded together and migrated further into the north country. These were people, according to the scriptures known as the Apocrypha, who sought a place of seclusion where they could be apart from the nations and live a life of their own.

"But they formed this plan for themselves," the record states, "that they would leave the multitude of nations and go to a more distant region, where mankind had never lived, that there at least they might keep their statutes which they had not kept in their own land." [48]

Although the apocryphal record is not universally recognized as canonized scripture, it is the single source that documents the departure of the lost tribes. And whereas many things in this volume of scripture have been confirmed as true and correctly translated[49], still the actuality of the alleged departure itself remains in question. Supplementary knowledge and information found in modern scripture, however, is enough to give it considerable credence and verification.

"And they went in by the narrow passages of the Euphrates River," the record continues. "For at that time the Most High performed signs for them and stopped the channels of the river until they had passed over. Through that region there was a long way to go, a journey of a year and a half; and that country is called Arzareth."[50]

Certainly there is a great deal of mystery and intrigue surrounding such an event. The time period and geographic location involved both blend together to give a historic background to a very unusual occurrence in Old Testament history. Considerable lore has accumulated over the years as to what actually happened to the ten lost tribes, or at least a certain part of them, and speculation sometimes has known no bounds concerning where they might be, or even if they still exist. Yet again in modern scripture there is additional information, some of which not only forecasts the tribes' eventual return but also hints at how they might have disappeared, in the first place, while in the country referred to as Arzareth many centuries ago.

"And they who are in the north countries shall come in remembrance before the Lord," modern scripture says, referring to when the tribes return, "and their prophets shall hear his voice and shall no longer stay themselves; and they shall smite the rocks, and the ice shall flow down at their presence. And an highway shall be cast up in the midst of the great deep."[51]

The return of the tribes, from whatever place it might be, will undoubtedly be a very miraculous occurrence, characterized by crumbling rocks and flowing ice, as well as a type of highway rising out of the sea. Also in comparison, and by implication, similar conditions and circumstances might have been present in the place called Arzareth at the time that the tribes originally disappeared.

Strange and significant things exist in connection with this group of people. First, there were the signs performed by the Most High when the tribes crossed the Euphrates River, followed by their disappearance into some remote and isolated area. Second, there is the prediction in scripture telling about prophets someday bringing the tribes out of obscurity through some kind of polar or arctic exit. Obviously it is a very unusual situation, not always typical of Israelite history, but at the same time not totally unexpected.

When Jesus visited the people in the Western Hemisphere, for example, soon after his resurrection, he told them that he would soon visit the tribes who were lost. Apparently they were unknown to any of the surrounding nations at that time. He reminded them, however, that they were not lost as far as he and his Father were concerned because they knew exactly where they were located.

"But now I go unto the Father," Jesus said on that occasion, "and also to show myself unto the lost tribes of Israel, for they are not lost unto the Father, for he knoweth whither he hath taken them."[52]

The implication was that following their arrival in Arzareth, the tribes had not remained in that area, being dispersed and sifted among the nations, but had gone to another region where they could definitely be apart by themselves. A further implication is that something extremely unusual occurred at that point which placed them in a completely new context and environment as far as history is concerned!

Just as the Most High, most likely Jehovah himself, had performed signs in order for the tribes to cross the Euphrates River, so now he performed other signs enabling them to enter a new area, unobserved and undetected by other groups of people but still remaining within the confines of the earth. It was his purpose, as well as that of his Father, to keep this particular group separate from the rest of the world, not permitting them to be scattered and intermingled with a non-Israelite population. For whatever reason, it had become their destiny to "leave the multitude of the nations and go to a more distant region, where mankind had never lived," there to remain until a time far distant during the latter days.53

In that future time, Jehovah will again perform signs for them, "and their prophets shall hear his voice and shall no longer stay themselves; and they shall smite the rocks, and the ice shall flow down at their presence." 54 And after all of this takes place, during an extremely important time in world history, the lost tribes of Israel will then make their way southward out of the north countries, having spent many centuries in seclusion, and once more join normal society and take their rightful place among the nations!

9

A FORGOTTEN PEOPLE

The most prominent opinion as to what happened to the Ten Tribes following their journey into the north country is that they settled in their new area and eventually dispersed among the nations. The results of a poll published in 1979, for example, stated that fifty-three per cent of the respondents favored this view. Twenty-nine per cent believed the tribes had been transported to another planet or sphere, much like the City of Enoch, while eleven per cent visualized them still in the north country, hidden away somewhere in the polar regions. Four per cent favored the idea of people living in a hollow earth, and the remainder had other theories of their own.[55]

In general, however, the dispersion theory was the most prevalent, as it continues to be, among those familiar with the subject of the lost tribes. Some have stated outright, in fact, that the tribes are actually not lost at all but merely unidentified, existing in a variety of places and being mixed and dispersed among different countries of the world. They are part of the Israelites whose purpose, according to the blessings of Abraham, is to be a strengthening influence in society and a leaven among the people.

Not only are the tribes unidentified, however, but in a sense also forgotten. After many centuries they are seldom recognized or discussed, if at all, and any mention of them anymore is more apt to be regarded as fiction than fact. The concept of the lost tribes, rather than being authentic, is often considered to be legendary and in the same kind of category as the lost city of Atlantis.

And yet it was not meant to be that way, as far as Jehovah was concerned. The tribes of Israel were intended to be lost and separated from one another, especially from those who were located in Palestine and Jerusalem, but not forgotten or regarded as legendary or non-existent. The Lord emphasized this while speaking to the Nephite people on the western Continent.

"And behold, this is the land of your inheritance," he told them, "and the Father hath given it unto you. And not at any time hath the Father given me commandment that I should tell it unto your brethren at Jerusalem. Neither at any time hath the Father given me commandment that I should tell unto them concerning the other tribes of the house of Israel, whom the Father hath led away out of the land."[56] The latter group, of course, definitely included the Ten Tribes.

Once again it was not just the Father but primarily Jehovah who led some of the tribes out of Assyrian captivity and into the north country. The indication also is that it was not a matter of them being taken to a place where they could disperse and mix with the nations, but rather to a location where they could be separate by themselves and exist independently.

And yet in reality, as far as a dispersion theory is concerned in regard to the lost tribes, it could be that such a theory, in part, is accurate after all. When the Assyrians conquered the Kingdom of Israel at the end of the eighth Century B.C., for example, the policy of the invader at that time was not to deport an entire population but only about one-half, or even less. Then by bringing in colonists from other parts of the empire to take their place, the new rulers could weaken the existing social structure and be able to maintain stronger control.[57]

The segment of population left behind in what had been the Kingdom of Israel continued on as before and after being mixed with incoming colonists from abroad eventually became known as the Samaritans, a hybrid people part Israelite and part otherwise. Approximately one half of the original ten tribes, in other words, were actually among those who became dispersed among the nations. But the important thing is that the other half was carried into Assyrian captivity, at least a part of which eventually broke away and was led by Jehovah and his Father into the north country, in which place they soon disappeared.

According to modern scripture, Jesus visited the lost tribes sometime after his visit to the Nephites. In what location he did not say, only that it was at a place definitely known to the Father. But one thing again appears certain, and that is that the people were still Israelites, not a hybrid group that had been merged with other nations.

"I am not sent but unto the lost sheep of the house of Israel," Jesus said.[58] This was true during his ministry in Palestine and also in his brief ministry among the Nephites. And the fact that he went in person to the lost tribes, wherever they might have been, is apparent evidence that they too were still pure Israelite in origin.

In whatever place the tribes exist right now, at least some of them are a religious people, and there are prophets among them.

These men, according to scripture, are temporarily staying themselves, waiting for the command to return from seclusion, at which time they will visit an American city called Zion, or the New Jerusalem, and there receive an important religious endowment at the hands of fellow Israelites.

"And there shall fall down and be crowned with glory," the scripture say, "even in Zion, by the hands of the servants of the Lord, even the children of Ephraim. And they shall be filled with songs of everlasting joy."[59] And at that point in time, after many hundreds of years of Israelite history, the Ten Tribes will again join normal society, and the saga of a forgotten people will finally come to an end!

10

IN BEHALF OF THE FATHER

Even though Jehovah is in charge of many things in the universe, including the creation itself, he always acts under the direction and influence of his Father. This was again evident on one occasion when he was speaking to Moses in the mount as though he were the Father, referring to the many worlds which he had created.

"And by the word of my power have I created them," he said, "which is mine Only Begotten Son, who is full of grace and truth. And worlds without number have I created; and I also created them for mine own purpose; and by the Son I created them, which is mine Only Begotten."

"The heavens, they are many," he continued, "and they cannot be numbered unto man; but they are numbered unto me, for they are mine. And as one earth shall pass away, and the heavens thereof, even so shall another come, and there is no end to my works, neither to my words."[60] Again it was the Son who was actually speaking, although according to how the scripture sounds, it would appear to be the Father.

Jehovah had many titles, the first of which was that of Firstborn, acquired when he came into the world of spirits and began his first estate. Upon entering mortality and a second estate, he also became the Only Begotten, the only human being on earth who was the offspring of a mortal mother as well as God the Father. It was by Jehovah, therefore, acting as the Only Begotten Son and through the supreme authority of his Father, that worlds in the universe are and have been created.

The reality of such was also verified on one occasion by Joseph Smith and a man named Sidney Rigdon, both of whom received an extraordinary vision and revelation. "And now, after the many testimonies which have been given of him," they said, referring to Jehovah, "this is the testimony, last of all, which we give of him: that he lives! For we saw him, even on the right hand of God; and we heard the voice bearing record that he is the Only Begotten of the Father, that by him, and through him, and of him, the worlds are and were created, and the inhabitants thereof are begotten sons and daughters unto God."[61]

Certainly there were many instances when Jehovah was the one who personally accomplished something, or received some type of commendation, yet he gave the glory and credit to his Father. When he led part of the ten tribes into the north country, for example, specifically to a location where they would be apart from surrounding nations, he spoke as if it were the Father who led or escorted them. But again the person in charge was Jehovah himself.

"For they are not lost unto the Father," he said at that time, "for he knoweth whither he hath taken them."[62]

It is standard protocol, and an established tradition inspired by heaven, that one conducting an event always acts under the auspices of a higher authority, especially when the latter is present, and even when not present. There is no greater example and precedent for this than in the mortal life and mission of Jehovah. In everything he did, he exemplified a complete submission to the authority, as well as the will, of the Father.

In this connection, there are again those instances when it appears to be the Father who is speaking or giving instructions, whereas in reality it is Jehovah. An example of this, as recorded in modern scripture, is when Jehovah delivered to the prophet Malachi certain well-known passages contained in the last two chapters of the Old Testament.

"Thus said the Father unto Malachi," Jesus said, speaking to the Nephites on the American Continent. "Behold, I will send my messenger, and he shall prepare the way before me, and the Lord whom ye seek shall suddenly come to his temple, even the messenger of the covenant, whom ye delight in; behold, he shall come, saith the Lord of Hosts."[63]

A few verses later the record confirms who it was that actually spoke to Malachi, namely Jehovah, the one who also spoke to the children of Israel in the wilderness and gave the Law of Moses on Mount Sinai: "Remember ye the law of Moses, my servant," he said, "which I commanded unto him in Horeb for all Israel, with the statutes and judgments."[64]

In some of the things that Jehovah says or does, therefore, it is as though the Father himself were speaking or acting through him. Regarding many of the Lord's statements and activities, this is the principle involved, whether during mortality, before or after.

During his mortal ministry in Jerusalem, Jesus alluded partially to this particular concept. "For I have not spoken of myself," he said, "but the Father which sent me, he gave me a commandment, what I should say, and what I should speak. And I know that his commandment is life everlasting: whatsoever I speak therefore, even as the Father said unto me, so I speak."[65]

Yet one of the notable exceptions to this principle was apparently when he made such statements as, "Not my will, but thine, be done," or "Not what I will, but what thou wilt." Especially in the Garden of Gethsemane the night before his death, these words appeared not to be prompted by his Father, nor those spoken earlier on the fateful day in premortality when he refused to side with Lucifer but instead approved of another plan.

"Father, thy will be done," Jehovah declared on that early occasion, "and the glory be thine forever."[66]

More likely these types of statements were made by the Lord in and of himself and consequently became a trademark of his divine being and personality, from the time of his primeval inception into the world of spirits as Firstborn to the crowning event of his atonement on earth, including the crucial times when he hesitated only for a moment to ask if there was any possibility that what lay ahead might in some ways be avoided. In all of these instances, however, he always verified and confirmed his earlier conviction: "Father, thy will be done, and the glory be thine forever!"

11

FOREORDINATION

In the realm of spirits, before the foundation of the world, Jehovah shared the status of Godhood with his Father. Together they formed what might be called a Quorum of Presidency in the universe. Eventually this quorum would comprise three members, but in the beginning it was apparently occupied solely by the Father and the Son.

Jehovah's presence in this august body stemmed from two previous foreordinations, first as "the firstborn among many brethren" in a first estate, and secondly as the future savior of mankind in a second estate, "the Lamb slain from the foundation of the world." Both of these ordinations were the result of obedience and achievement beginning as far back as an early sphere of intelligence.

The foreordinations of Jehovah, therefore, were occurrences of the greatest magnitude, having eternal consequences. But they were also precursor to many similar ones acquired by others which had their own impact upon the affairs of heaven, as well as later on earth during world history.

Along with Jehovah, for example, there were those who had been worthy and able in the state of intelligence, identities not only competent intellectually but also excelling in obedience and spirituality. These were the types of people that the Lord later acknowledged as spirits, referring to them as the noble and great ones that he would make rulers during a future time on earth. These were people such as Abraham, whom Jehovah mentioned specifically, but undoubtedly many others, a great host of men and women, in fact, who were selected ahead of time as individuals to be called to future positions of trust and leadership. Indeed, these were people that Jehovah and his Father would depend on to promote righteousness and carry out the plan of heaven, the ones whose mission on earth would be to represent the House of Israel as they had done earlier in premortality.

In the Bible this type of selection and preparation is called predestination, the naming of someone in advance who is to be called to a certain job or position. Another name, and one less likely to be misinterpreted, is foreordination, or in one sense ordination. The latter was the case when the Lord spoke to Jeremiah at one time and told him how he as a future prophet had been selected.

"Before I formed thee in the belly I knew thee," he said, "and before thou camest forth out of the womb I sanctified thee, and I ordained thee a prophet unto the nations."[67]

Thus it was that people in the world of spirits were selected and prepared, one at a time, to assume certain positions and responsibilities upon transfer to earth. Beginning with Jehovah, who was foreordained and called to be the Firstborn and also the future Redeemer, a huge cadre of responsible and qualified individuals, both men and women, were designated in the same manner, being given the important mandate of representing the Father and the Son in carrying out heaven's plan.

Consequently, this process was necessarily accomplished in three different stages: First, there was the predestination or foreordination of the individual involved. Second, a formal calling was given to him or her, an election to a particular job or position. Third, in order to finalize things, and for an ultimate and complete circumstance to be obtained, the person then needed to be chosen or formerly accepted, in addition to being called. In this manner the process of foreordination, election, and the act of choosing all took place in a proper sequence.

Regarding the time that Jehovah was chosen to be the Firstborn, along with those who immediately followed him, the scriptures generally give the same description. "For whom he did foreknow," the text says, referring to God and Jehovah, "he also did predestinate (foreordain) to be conformed to the image of his Son, that he might be the firstborn among many brethren. Moreover, whom he did predestinate, them he also called, and whom he called, them he also justified, and whom he justified, them he also glorified."[68]

Being foreordained and then called to a position, therefore, is never completely consummated until it is justified. This is a principle ordained in heaven and is operative on earth as well as in premortal life. It is one that applies especially to people with an Israelite connection or background, those who because of spirituality and good works earn preferential treatment in their transfer to earth but later do not always carry through and live up to expectations.

As an example, such was obviously the case among the twelve sons of Jacob, or Israel, although probably true also of many before that time, so-called Israelites coming from premortality between the time of Adam down to the time of Abraham. But it was noticeably true of some of Jacob's sons, men who helped originate the twelve tribes that eventually became known as the House of Israel.

Reuben, for instance, who was the firstborn, showed signs of good character at first but later broke an important law of chastity, thus forfeiting his right to the birthright. Other sons also acted irresponsibly. The most flagrant action of all, however, was when most of them planned to kill their younger brother Joseph because of jealousy but instead ended up selling him into Egypt. It was definitely not the ideal way of introducing the House of Israel as an institution on earth.

Certainly it became obvious from the beginning that people with an apparent foreordination and calling were not always successful. The trouble which Moses had with the rebellious children of Israel as they journeyed through the wilderness toward a promised land is a further example. Later there were also the disappointments of Saul, David, and Solomon, followed by more than three centuries of Israelite waywardness and idolatry, after which the House of Israel as an earthly institution finally came to a close. There were many good people living during those time periods, but again it is obvious that there were many also who did not live up to what was expected of them.

"For they are not all Israel which are of Israel," the Bible says, implying that the status acquired by certain people during a previous lifetime had been forfeited, or at least jeopardized, because of irresponsibility on earth.[69] Or such a scripture might also refer to people who were not Israelites in the first place. Even though some had been born into an Israelite lineage, in other words, they had never actually belonged to the original House of Israel. For whatever reason, different backgrounds from a previous lifetime might have been mixed with one another.

This type of situation is suggested when an individual such as Cain, with no evidence of previous spirituality, was born into the family of Adam and Eve. The same could be true in the family of Abraham when Ishmael, the firstborn, was born to one wife, but the second child Isaac was born to another. In this second instance, the implication is that Ishmael was originally not of the House of Israel, and consequently his life experience on earth was much different from that of Isaac, who became a great prophet and patriarch and whose status in premortality is unquestionable. Reference to Isaac and Ishmael, therefore, is especially significant.

"Neither because they are the seed of Abraham are they all children," the scripture says, "but in Isaac shall thy seed be called."

People regarded as the seed of Abraham, those born into his lineage, are heirs to certain blessings as outlined in biblical scripture. Yet at the same time, there are two significant subdivisions of his posterity, the one pertaining to the descendants of Isaac, and the other to descendants of Ishmael and Abraham's other children.

The first of these are called the children of promise, whereas the others are not.

"They which are the children of the flesh, these are not the children of God: but the children of the promise are counted for the seed."[70]

In the Bible, as well as in modern scripture, it tells a great deal about the patriarch Abraham, and especially about his relationship with Jehovah, how initially he left his home in Ur of the Chaldees and journeyed with his family to Haran near the land of Caanan. Prior to that time, the Lord spoke to him on at least one occasion, declaring that he had an important work for him to do, one that would take him to places he had never seen.

"Abraham, Abraham, behold, my name is Jehovah," he said, "and I have heard thee, and have come down to deliver thee, and to take thee away from thy father's house, and from all thy kinsfolk, into a strange land which thou knowest not of."[71]

It was in Haran that the Lord again spoke with Abraham, giving him new information, which was that in his seed, or by way of his descendants, all nations of the earth would be blessed. He would be the one, he told him, through whom all of the earth's families would receive "the blessings of salvation, even of life eternal."[72]

Once more it was Jehovah speaking. "And I will make of thee a great nation," he said, "and I will bless thee, and make thy name great; and thou shalt be a blessing: and I will bless them that bless thee, and curse him that curseth thee: and in thee shall all families of the earth be blessed."[73]

On several different occasions, God reiterated these same promises, not only to Abraham but also to Isaac and Jacob. Especially during the lifetime of these three great patriarchs was the will of heaven made known to men. The Abrahamic Covenant, was offered potentially to all mankind, both inside the House of Israel and without, extended to all who would obey the commandments and were willing to be gathered. The doctrine of Israelite membership by adoption, taught especially by the Apostle Paul following the death of Jesus and his resurrection, became a virtual door of opportunity for an untold number of people.

More and more it became increasingly apparent how important it was for one not only to be called but also chosen, not just to be elected but also justified. Regardless of previous success and past performance, the significant accomplishment often turned out to be what an individual could eventually make of himself, or herself, improving in spirituality and consistently profiting from experience. In many cases, in regard to human effort and expectations, it was a matter of the first ending up last, and the last first.

Ultimately for each person, there will come the time when he or she must stand on the quality of a mission accomplished and the type of record recorded. It will be a question of whether one has failed to live up to expectations or ended up fulfilling or exceeding them. There will be the time not only of calling, in other words, but also that of choosing.

"There has been a day of calling," the scripture says, "but the time has come for a day of choosing; and let those be chosen that are worthy."[74]

Unfortunately, as far as Israelites are concerned, and undoubtedly many other groups along the way, it appears to be characteristic of life experience and human nature that opportunities can be extended to many, but proportionately very few worthy responses are given in return. It is the idea often expressed in scripture that "many be called, but few chosen."[75] Many are given a chance to be successful in life, but many fail to live up to potential.

As a consequence, all down through history, from the time of Adam to Abraham, to Moses and the House of Israel, and then to New Testament times and the latter days, people who were favored by heaven and given a specific ordination and calling have made their way across a vast landscape and many centuries of time. Many others of different lineages and destinies accompanied them. Some were successful in their appointed times and places, and some were not, but eventually a vast vanguard of people finally arrived at the far edge of normal existence, and there on the threshold of a coming Millennium, they stopped for a time and waited. Not everyone was aware of what was happening, but they waited nevertheless upon the Lord and upon the will of Jehovah and his Father!

12

THE DIVINE MINISTRY

The advent of Jehovah into mortality is well known and documented, from the time of his birth in Bethlehem to the early years in Nazareth. Foreordained and called to be the future Messiah, he was the one chosen to represent the Father, on earth as well as in heaven, and from the very beginning he was in a dual role as the Only Begotten Son of Deity and also a member of the Godhead, the creator of heaven and earth.

And yet there was a small space of time when a veil was temporarily drawn between him and his Father, a veil already becoming thin when he was at the temple in Jerusalem at the age of twelve talking with learned men and doctors. His statement to his parents at that time that he needed to be about his Father's business was a clear indication that he already knew much about his calling and previous existence.

But as to what age he was actually aware of his identity as Jehovah, no one knows, and there are no clues in scripture except that as a child he "grew and waxed strong in spirit, filled with wisdom: and the grace of God was upon him." Also during his teenage years, he "increased in wisdom and stature, and in favor with God and man."[76]

It was inevitable, of course, long before the child was twelve years old, that he would learn about Jehovah. Through his knowledge of scripture, as well as instruction from parents and clergy, the name of this particular individual, would be familiar to him. Although the name became less common in scripture at a later time, it still would have been very recognizable to Jesus.

In present-day biblical scripture, there are only four references to Jehovah, those found in the Books of Exodus and Psalms, in addition to two in Isaiah. In the Book of Genesis, there is also the name Jehovah-Jireh, referring to the place in the land of Moriah where Abraham prepared to offer his son Isaac as a sacrifice.77

It must have been especially significant for Jesus to learn of the relationship between Abraham and his son Isaac, and that such a momentous event had occurred in the place known as Jehovah-jireh. At a very early age, he undoubtedly felt some kind of kinship with Abraham's son as he lay upon the altar, knowing how he must have felt and being glad that things turned out the way they did. There might have also been a presentiment of something for him personally, a prelude to other images and impressions of what would occur in the future.

Certainly it would be interesting and important to know what it was that happened during Jesus' teenage years, particularly between the ages of twelve and eighteen. It is very possible that he already knew how his life blended with that of Jehovah. This also presents the question of what he would have been doing during the twelve years preceding his actual ministry.

It is probably no coincidence that Jesus waited until his thirtieth year to begin teaching, since that was the age according to Jewish law when someone could assume the responsibilities of clergy, and even though he was not bound by such a restriction, he possibly wanted to avoid criticism by not openly opposing tradition. In any case, there was a significant amount of time during which he was noticeably inactive, as far as any reference in scripture is concerned, and assuming that by age thirty he was definitely aware of his identity with Jehovah, there is again the important question concerning some of his adult years.

Indeed, nothing in scripture provides a definite answer, either as to his whereabouts during this time period or what kind of communication he might have had with his Father. All that can be stated with any certainty is that when he eventually appeared before John the Baptist in order to be baptized, coming from the city of Nazareth, from somewhere in the desert, or from whatever area, he was "about thirty years of age" and ready to begin his ministry. It was finally that time in history when everything had been accomplished preparatory to the formal advent of the Messiah, a time when the Father himself would now speak personally from heaven and introduce the world to his Son.

"And Jesus, when he was baptized, went up straightway out of the water: and lo the heavens were opened unto him, and he saw the Spirit of God descending like a dove, and landing upon him: and lo a voice from heaven, saying, This is my beloved Son, in whom I am well pleased."[78]

In the beginning, when Adam and Eve were in the Garden of Eden, it was always the Father who spoke to them and gave them commandments. After the event known as The Fall, however, when they were driven from his presence, the Father's role devolved upon Jehovah, who subsequently became his advocate and intermediary. This meant that whenever God spoke to man after that time, as recorded in scripture, it was Jehovah who was speaking, the one exception being the thirty-three years that Jesus spent on earth as a mortal performing his second estate, at which time the Father temporarily again directed the affairs of mankind.

Following the introduction of his Son at the time of baptism, for example, there were at least two other times when He intervened and spoke audibly from heaven, once on the Mount of Transfiguration, and again at a later time when certain Greeks came to worship at Jerusalem during the Feast of the Passover.[79]

In addition, there were undoubtedly other occasions when the Son heard from his Father during those years, corresponding personally with him. And along with such private interviews, there was the communication provided by way of angels and other ministrants. One of these times was during the forty days that Jesus spent in seclusion in the desert immediately following his baptism.

"And he was there in the wilderness forty days, tempted of Satan," the scripture reveals, "and was with the wild beasts; and the angels ministered unto him."[80]

On many occasions throughout his ministry, the Lord appears to have been fully aware of his identification with Jehovah. During the twelve years before he talked to John, or even earlier, it was apparently made known to him who he really was, the conversations with his Father being enough to remove any questions he might have had. And at times such as when he raised the daughter of Jairus from the dead and calmed the storm raging across the sea of Galilee, the time when his disciples remarked that "even the winds and the sea" obeyed him, Jesus without question knew the full truth.

At any stage during the last three years of his life, he had all power given to him by the Father, even to lay down his life voluntarily and immediately take it up again. Within himself he had the ability to do anything that the Father could do. Indeed, he was Jehovah as he had been before, but now with a body of flesh and bones, he could relinquish mortal life at any time and theoretically in an instant gain immortality. Again he was the Son, as he had always been, continually promoting the cause of heaven and acting in consort with his Father.

13

A CONCEPT OF DEITY

While speaking to people in Jerusalem and Palestine, Jesus often referred to his Father. This was disconcerting to many of the Jews, and because of it, they accused him of blasphemy. But he tolerated their accusations and continued to emphasize a Father and Son relationship. "I seek not my own will," he told them, "but the will of the Father which hath sent me." [81]

"Where is thy Father?" they asked on one occasion. Jesus replied, "Ye neither know me, nor my Father: if ye had known me, ye should have known my Father also."[82]

Jesus made almost this exact statement to his apostles at one time, when he said, "If ye had known me, ye should have known my Father also: and from henceforth ye know him, and have seen him." It was then that Philip said unto him, "Lord, shew us the Father, and it sufficeth us."

Jesus answered, "Have I been so long time with you, and yet hast thou not known me, Philip? He that hath seen me hath seen the Father; and how sayest thou then, shew us the Father?"[83]

Surely it was a poetic way, and an accurate way, of saying who God the Father was and what he looked like. The apostles were all well acquainted with Jesus by now, and with this familiarity they should have been able to visualize his Father, something of his general appearance, and what kind of person he was. In other words, he was not only a separate individual, but someone with a physical body, in form and appearance like Jesus himself.

In reference to Seth, the son of Adam, the scripture says, "And Adam lived an hundred and thirty years and begat a son in his own likeness and image, and called his name Seth."[84] An additional comment in modern scripture also says that "he (Seth) was a perfect man, and his likeness was the express likeness of his father, insomuch that he seemed to be like unto his father in all things and could be distinguished from him only by his age."[85]

Whereas much of the world today regards Deity not as a man, but rather as an ethereal essence of some kind, Jesus nevertheless was not hesitant to say that he and his Father were very much alike, so much so that people, might not be able to tell them apart. In essence, he was telling Philip that when the day *did* come that he met the Father in person, the experience should not come as a surprise.

At an earlier time, Jesus had also told the people, "He that believeth on me believeth not on me but on him that sent me. And he that seeth me seeth him that sent me."[86]

He also expressed things a different way by saying, "I and my Father are one."[87] Yet in this latter instance, so that people would not misinterpret him and think that he meant two personalities incorporated into one individual, he declared, "And the glory which thou gavest me I have given them," referring to his Father. And of the apostles he said, "that they may be one, even as we are one: I in them, and thou in me, . . . that they may be made perfect in one; and that the world may know that thou hast sent me, and hast loved them, as thou hast loved me."[88] He emphasized that the apostles should be one in mind and purpose, just as were he and his Father.

Indeed, throughout the world today there is no such unity among people, but in its place there is a multitude of religious creeds and beliefs, especially concerning the nature of God. It is not just a question about God the Father himself, whether he is some kind of spirit essence or an actual person with a body, but also about his relationship with Jehovah, His Son. Are they in actuality two separate personalities with individual bodies? Or is it true that it is more definitive and complex than that, namely that the Father is God, as is also the Son, and yet they are not two separate individuals with bodies of their own but two spiritual personalities who in some way are incorporated into one?

The same might be said of the Holy Spirit or Holy Ghost when speaking of the Trinity or Godhead. The Holy Ghost is God, in other words, a functional part of the Trinity, and yet along with the other two members, are the three of them three different Gods with separate bodies? Or are they three personalities who in some way are joined or consolidated in one person?

Certainly a particular doctrine, principle, or philosophy could be familiar and comprehensible to one individual yet not understandable to another. This is to be expected when people from different cultures, value systems, and religious backgrounds come together. Very often it depends on what someone has learned and internalized while growing into adulthood. Until a unity of the faith is someday accomplished, the important thing is for there to be patience and tolerance, as well as a willingness to respect another's point of view. In the meantime the search for truth can continue.

And although it has been shown many times that it is often fruitless to try to prove things by way of discussion and quoting scripture, still the question asked by Philip long ago is one that a person in a modern setting might very well ask today. "Show us the Father," in other words, "and it will suffice us."

It is well known that at the time of the Creation, God said, "Let us make man in our image, after our likeness."[89] These are his exact words, and at first glance, the meaning would appear to be unmistakable. Just as Adam "begat a son in his own likeness, after his image, and called his name Seth," for example, so God the Father apparently did likewise.

It might be theorized, therefore, that the best way to know what Adam looked like, especially when he allegedly could be distinguished from Seth only by age, was merely to look at Seth. In a similar way, it could be said that the best way to know what God looks like today is to visualize Adam!

According to this same kind of reasoning, it should be possible in a modern setting to visualize the God of the universe, in a very general sense, merely by looking at another human being. Is it presumptuous and disrespectful to suggest such a thing? Of course, it could not be just any human being, but one that general opinion regards as an optimum or ideal, some figure within whatever culture or society that qualifies as a model person or utopian-type individual. If it were indeed possible to obtain such an image in this way, reality concerning God might more closely be approached than by visualizing him as some undefined essence or omnipotent power that often seems remote and impersonal.

It still might be said, however, that no one will ever really know what God looks like until someone actually sees him personally. And such an event, as recorded in the Bible, has never taken place since He talked with Adam and Eve in the Garden of Eden. Subsequent to that time, it has only been Jehovah who has dealt with mankind and made an occasional personal appearance.

But men and women at any time in the earth's history, even with little or no knowledge of Deity, still might not be mistaken in visualizing God as a man, a glorified being who long ago passed through the resurrection and along with Jehovah is now guiding the affairs of the universe. Joseph Smith and Lorenzo Snow, the two men who introduced the unique doctrine concerning God and man, stating that "as man now is, God once was," would undoubtedly agree with this kind of reasoning. Both were familiar with things of a highly spiritual nature and had religious experiences almost beyond comprehension.

In one such experience, for example, which pertained only to Joseph Smith, two members of the Godhead, for whatever purpose, and for the first time since the Garden of Eden, reportedly appeared to a man on earth. It was the first time in the world's regular history that anyone had seen both the Father and the Son together and talked with them, as one man would speak to another. It is also the one specific event, if it can be accepted by faith, that can forever answer the question of what God actually looks like and whether or not he is a person separate and distinct from his Son Jehovah!

The event in question is one that has been reported many times, although still unknown to most of the world's population. A description of it was given very briefly, and in the words of Joseph Smith himself, several years after it had occurred in the year 1820.

It was an event that took place in a forest not far from Joseph's home in western New York. He was just a young man at the time, and his object in going to a secret place to pray one day was to ask which church he should join. He said it was the first time he had ever tried to pray vocally, and although he had faith that the prayer would be answered, he was undoubtedly surprised at what actually happened.

After certain things occurred, he said, which temporarily discouraged him and for a time caused him to feel that he was "doomed to utter destruction," he eventually witnessed a miraculous vision, one that changed his life and gave him an entirely new viewpoint and perspective concerning Deity.

"I saw a pillar of light exactly over my head," he related, "above the brightness of the sun, which descended gradually until it fell upon me."

"I saw two Personages, whose brightness and glory defy all description, standing above me in the air. One of them spake unto me, calling me by name and said, pointing to the other—This is my Beloved Son. Hear Him!"[90]

Regardless of a person's race, nationality, religion, or any worldly condition or circumstance, this one event among all others, if it can be accepted as accurate and true, was a final confirmation that the Father and the Son are two separate individuals, having resurrected bodies of flesh and bones and being intimately involved in the affairs of mankind. This one event alone, especially in view of information which Joseph Smith received at the time, was not only a valuable commentary on the concept of Deity and the nature of God but also a unique announcement to the people of the world. Occurring at the beginning of what came to be known as the Dispensation of the Fulness of Times, it initiated an entirely new era of human history and heralded many significant events yet to come!

14

AN EARTHLY MISSION

Jehovah made it clear from the beginning of his earthly ministry that he had been sent to earth by his Father. He said many times that he did not speak in and of himself but always in behalf of the one who had sent him.

Jesus Christ also told people that by receiving him personally, they were in effect receiving the Father, and by implication, the opposite would be true whenever they refused to believe the Son. Although the two were separate individuals, they were nevertheless one in unity and purpose, and to accept or disapprove of one was essentially to do the same for the other.

"He that receiveth you receiveth me," he said to the twelve apostles at the time they were called to the ministry, "and he that receiveth me receiveth him that sent me."[91]

In sending Jehovah to the earth, the Father in actuality was sending his Son on a mission. Just as Church authorities in a modern setting send a young man or woman into the mission field to preach the gospel, so the God of the universe sent his Only Begotten Son to do the same. Again an important precedent or example was established, one that had already been followed in previous times, and one also to be observed in the future.

In this connection, the Gospel of John in the New Testament begins by saying, "In the beginning was the Word, and the Word was with God, and the Word was God. The same was in the beginning with God."[92]

Another way of saying this, however, is by way of a paraphrase and parallel translation as recorded in modern scripture: "In the beginning was the gospel preached through the Son. And the gospel was the word, and the word was with the Son, and the Son was with God, and the Son was of God. The same was in the beginning with God."[93]

Certainly the main reason that Jesus came to earth, other than performing the infinite atonement, was to preach the gospel. During his brief ministry of three years, there were many cities he had to visit and messages he needed to give. On one occasion when he went into the desert and the people followed to ask that he stay with them, he answered that there were still other places he had to go. "I must preach the kingdom of God to other cities also," he said, "for therefore am I sent."[94]

Such matters were undoubtedly discussed by Jesus and his Father before his mission began. Different policies and procedures were reviewed, as well as itineraries of travel. Of primary importance was the specific group of people that were to hear his message. "I am not sent but unto the lost sheep of the house of Israel," he said at one time, and as far as the gospel was concerned, the same kind of restriction was temporarily placed upon the apostles.[95]

The idea that Jehovah was sent to earth as a missionary, therefore, representing not only his Father but also the Kingdom of Heaven, is a true concept. And as such, Jesus himself might be regarded not only as a missionary but also as an Apostle.

The word "apostle," by derivation, is said to be the equivalent of the Greek word "apostolos," referring to a messenger, ambassador, or one who is sent. He is someone who speaks or acts not of himself, but as one representing a higher power. In this sense, the term apostle consequently signifies a servant rather than a superior. Paul in the New Testament had this in mind when he spoke of Jesus as "the Apostle and High Priest of our profession."[96]

As one sent from the presence of the Father, Jesus certainly was the epitome of someone who is not just a missionary, a messenger, or an ambassador, but one especially dedicated above everything else in carrying out the will of a superior or benefactor. In all that he did, he recognized that he had been commissioned and sent to do the work of the one who had sent him. No greater example can be given of respect and commitment, as well as of an ideal Father and Son relationship!

It was also Jesus who reminded the people that he and his Father were one. What one did, he said, the other always supported and sanctioned. Regardless of public attitude and opinion in relation to the Son, the same would be shared by the Father, who regarded words and actions as being either complimentary or intended as an affront.

Just as those who received Jesus also received the one who had commissioned him, it was the same in a variety of other instances. "He that believeth on me," for example, "believeth not on me, but on him that sent me."[97] "He that honoreth not the Son honoreth not the Father which hath sent him."[98] "Whosoever shall deny me before men, him will I also deny before my Father which is in heaven."[99]

But a more flagrant instance was something Jesus said to seventy of his disciples before sending them forth on missions of their own. "He that heareth you heareth me," he said, "and he that despiseth you despiseth me; and he that despisest me despisest him that sent me."[100] Obviously the reference to such a word as "despise," which in turn was reflected upon the Father, is an extreme example of how serious negative reactions to Jesus or his disciples could be.

Again it was a solemn declaration, not only for those who might hear the words of the apostles or disciples, but for anyone to whom the gospel might be taught. At any given time the implication of such statements would continue to have an effect through the centuries. Indeed they would be a reminder to people everywhere, depending on knowledge and understanding, that they must eventually submit to the will of the Father and accept his son Jehovah. Not only would it be important in their lives upon the earth, but their future in the eternities would depend on it.

"I have glorified thee on the earth," Jesus prayed to his Father shortly before he died. "I have finished the work which thou gavest me to do." And then he reaffirmed the inevitable message which everyone in the world must hear someday and understand: "And this is life eternal, that they might know thee the only true God and Jesus Christ whom thou hast sent!"[101]

15

A FATHER'S TUTELAGE

As a mortal, yet at the same time the Son of God, Jesus told the people in Jerusalem and Palestine that he had many things to tell them, all of which he had previously heard from his Father. During his ministry he said that he did not speak in and of himself but spoke only of that which he had been taught. Again and again, this was the basic principle in his missionary work, and his main purpose was to carry out his Father's will and to please Him.

He also said that he could do nothing of himself except the things which he had actually seen his Father do. It was not just a matter of someone teaching and explaining to a son, but showing and demonstrating as well. At least such is the implication in scripture. The idea was that an effective teacher teaches not by word only but by example.

"The Son can do nothing of himself, but what he seeth the Father do," Jesus said. "For what things soever he doeth, these also doeth the Son likewise."

A short time earlier, Jesus had miraculously healed a man at the Pool of Bethesda in Jerusalem, and because it was the Sabbath Day, he was criticized for it. But again he answered his critics by referring to his

Father. "For the Father loveth the Son," he told them, "and sheweth him all things that himself doeth: and he will shew him greater works than these, that ye may marvel."[102]

Surely there was a multitude of greater works and miracles that Jesus alluded to, events which testified of divine tutelage by his Father. The healing of those plagued with blindness and leprosy was especially impressive, as was also the restoration to health of people possessed with devils and evil spirits. Knowledge of these types of ailments and the power and authority necessary to cure them were undoubtedly all part of the Lord's premortal education.

Events such as calming the sea, walking on water, and feeding thousands of people on two separate occasions with only a plateful of food are all events and actions which bespeak prior knowledge and instruction, the kind which could only be provided by God himself. Again it was an education that came from a divine parent, one who in reality was instructing his Son and preparing him for a mission.

But the most impressive thing was the premortal preparation which pertained to life and death, the ability and power instilled by the Father into the Son to control death itself! "For as the Father raiseth up the dead, and quickeneth them," Jesus said, "even so the Son quickeneth whom he will."[103]

Although the Lord's remarks at this time might have applied mainly to the coming resurrection, when he would have power not only to raise himself from the dead but also others, the "greater works" mentioned earlier could have also included instances when Jesus brought people back to life during mortality. The events concerning the son of the widow of Nain, the daughter of Jairus, and in particular Lazarus, the brother of Mary and Martha, were certainly among the greatest of all the miracles which Jesus performed during his ministry. In addition to these, there were possibly still others not mentioned in scripture.

But in regard to the resurrection itself, which was the single most important event in history, along with the atonement that preceded it, Jesus stated clearly ahead of time what would take place. "Therefore doth my Father love me," he told the Jewish people, "because I lay down my life, that I might take it again. No man taketh it from me, but I lay it down of myself." And then he told them something no one had ever heard before. "I have power to lay it down," he said, "and I have power to take it again. This commandment have I received of my Father."[104]

Earlier he had told the Jews basically the same thing when he said that three days after the destruction of the temple, he would raise it up again, although at the time they misunderstood what he meant. And even on later occasions, when he talked with his apostles concerning his coming death and resurrection, they themselves still did not completely understand.

Jehovah knew exactly what was involved in the phenomenon of death and the resurrection, not only because he had been instructed in it but in some unexplainable way he had witnessed it as it had occurred in the lifetime of his Father. Again he told the people, "The Son can do nothing of himself, but what he seeth the Father do: for what things soever he doeth, these also doeth the Son likewise."[105]

Joseph Smith, who along with Lorenzo Snow taught that God preceded Jehovah in mortality and went through the same type of life experiences, made certain statements at one time which shed important light upon this particular scripture. "As the Father hath power in Himself," he said, "even so hath the Son power—to do what? Why, what the Father did. The answer is obvious—in a manner to lay down his body and take it up again. Jesus, what are you going to do? To lay down my life as my Father did, and take it up again."

Joseph continued, "What did Jesus do? Why, I do the things I saw my Father do when worlds came rolling into existence. My Father worked out his kingdom with fear and trembling, and I must do the same; and when I get my kingdom, I shall present it to my Father, so that he may obtain kingdom upon kingdom, and it will exalt him in glory. He will then take a higher exaltation, and I will take his place, and thereby become exalted myself."[106] In this manner Jehovah was thus following in his Father's footsteps, as it were, being the heir apparent of his glory and kingdom.

It is uncertain as to what kind of inferences should be drawn from these types of statements. The implication, of course, is that the Father at one time exercised the power which he had to raise himself from mortality and death to immortality by way of the resurrection. Like the Son who would come after him, he obtained the keys of the resurrection which then gave him the authority and power to resurrect other people.

Yet in regard to the Father, there is definitely the question as to whether or not there was an atonement and physical sacrifice involved, even a crucifixion or something like unto it. Such a thing is implied although nothing in contemporary religion or public opinion verifies such a thing. But the implication is there, especially when Jesus said that he did nothing except what he had seen his Father do.

Consequently, if scriptural implication and the statements of Joseph Smith are accurate, and if it were possible for someone to see God the Father today, it might well be that he would see not only a glorified person with a physical body of flesh and bones but one also where the identifying prints of crucifixion nails were in his hands and feet, as well as in those of Jehovah!

16

ANIMAL SACRIFICE

It would be interesting to know what Jesus thought, as a child and young man growing up in Palestine, when he saw the long rows of crucified figures hanging on crosses along the highways where the Romans had placed them. Similar to telephone poles in a modern setting, the crosses sometimes stretched for miles, advertising the consequences of violating the laws of the empire and impressing on people's minds how important it was to obey the emperor. Growing up in Nazareth and traveling periodically to passover feasts in Jerusalem, Jesus could not help but be offended by the scene and very possibly had a presentiment that the cross someday would involve him personally.

In regard to the Romans, it is said that they themselves found crucifixion to be a distasteful form of punishment, but effective nevertheless as a deterrent to crime and disobedience. By displaying criminals in this manner, positioning them along busy highways and at prominent intersections, the use of the cross provided a convenient and effective method of crime control.

Still, there was a natural aversion to the penalty among civilized people, and the fact that it turned out to be the punishment for Jehovah was a sacrilegious irony.

This type of activity, therefore, even as it pertains to animals and when regarded religiously, can certainly be viewed as a distasteful practice. It is doubtful that over the course of centuries, people actually enjoyed taking the life of a lamb, ram, or bullock, or whatever animal, for the purpose of a religious ordinance. Yet in order for the thousands, even millions, of sacrifices to occur and be symbolic, they necessarily contained certain elements, including the shedding of innocent blood.

Again, Jesus must have thought of such things, especially when he read in scripture how Abraham dreaded taking a certain life, not of an animal, but of his son Isaac. Surely he might have wondered if there was another way of doing things. He knew well enough that animal sacrifice was a divine commandment, and that it had a purpose, yet in reading about the final moments in the compelling drama pertaining to Isaac, and reacting to them in a young boy's mind, there still would be some hope that somehow God would intervene and indeed say there was another way.

Little did the Romans know that someday some of them also would be confronted with these same types of feelings, realizing that an event of inestimable magnitude was taking place on a hilltop outside Jerusalem at the place of crucifixion! In the meantime, however, another drama continued to unfold, one having greater import in history as well as tragic consequences.

Certainly it is difficult to visualize the significance and extent of animal sacrifices down through the centuries. Within the context of Hebrew and Israelite history alone, trying to comprehend the volume of religious ceremonies and activity that took place is overwhelming. One example is an account given by Josephus, the ancient Jewish historian, who states that at a single passover in Jerusalem, 256,500 lambs were slain to serve as religious sacrifices. This was a huge event, even if it took days to accomplish the task because of the large number of people involved.[107]

The enormity of animal sacrifices on such occasions, occurring over and over at many different times and places throughout history, again draws attention to the tremendous importance of this type of activity. Without question it was one of the most significant practices of the ancient world. And at the very center of things, especially as far as Christianity is concerned, was the presence of Jehovah as a creator in the universe and the Son of God during mortality. His atonement and personal sacrifice, occurring at the end of his earthly ministry, was undoubtedly the most important event in all of history.

The account of the Lord's atonement, consisting of the time that He spent in the Garden of Gethsemane, as well as when he was punished by the Jews and crucified on Calvary, is well known to many millions of people worldwide. Christians and those of other faiths are well acquainted with the life of Jesus and how he died upon the cross.

And yet something that is not so well known, and in fact very seldom mentioned or publicized, is the idea that animal sacrifice itself was not only important anciently but inherently is still an important part of religion. In conjunction with other forms of sacrifice, it is not just a significant religious ordinance that dates back to the past but one that will again be practiced in the future, very prominently for a time and basically in the same way that it was transacted in ancient times.

For thousands of years, people of the ancient world brought sacrifices to their gods and placed them upon the altar. Those who did so for Jehovah, and who understood the true meaning of what they did, knew that God would someday come down in person and offer himself as the infinite and final sacrifice, infinite in that it would be the supreme offering, and final in that it would signal the end of the Law of Moses.

Again it was Jehovah who had given the Law in the first place, and following his death it was he also who gave notice that it had come to an end, including the discontinuation of animal sacrifices. "And ye shall offer up unto me no more the shedding of blood," he said, speaking to the people known as the Nephites. "Yea, your sacrifices and your burnt offerings shall be done away, for I will accept none of your sacrifices and your burnt offerings."

Then he told them of a new type of sacrifice they could make, one that would be part of his fulfilment of the Mosaic Law and a continuing offering for centuries to come. "And ye shall offer for a sacrifice unto me a broken heart," he said, "and a contrite spirit."[108] All in all, it was a new concept, patterned after teachings such as those found in the Sermon on the Mount.

Sometime later he also introduced into Nephite society a new type of sacrament, one that he had given to his twelve apostles on the occasion of the Last Supper. It was the idea that by partaking of bread and wine in a sacred religious ceremony, however simple it might be, people could show a remembrance for what Jesus had done for them in his Atonement, at the same time bringing an acceptable offering before him in the form of a broken heart and a contrite spirit. Once more it was the type of ordinance that could be repeated many times, a continuing expression of sacrifice that would benefit people personally and prepare them for a future entrance into the Kingdom of Heaven.

Yet again, as far as animal sacrifice is concerned, which has now been dormant in Christianity for centuries, such activity still has an important function and purpose in religion that is yet to be accomplished. It is a principle pertaining to the period of time known as the last days, as well as to the so-called Dispensation of the Fulness of Times. Specifically it refers to the idea in scripture which states that as part of a "restitution of all things," it will be the purpose of the Lord "that in the dispensation of the fulness of times he might gather together in one all things in Christ, both which are in heaven, and which are on earth."[109]

All of the principles and ordinances of the gospel which were introduced and practiced during former dispensations, in other words, those relating to Adam, Enoch, Noah, Abraham, Moses, and Jesus Christ, will during a seventh and final dispensation be restored and practiced as part of a preparation for the Second Coming and the beginning of the Millennium. All basic aspects of true religion, including animal sacrifice, will be reintroduced, or introduced for the first time, during a grand program of restoration.

At a time when a huge temple complex is built in the central part of the United States, accompanying the construction of a new city called Zion, or the New Jerusalem, many important things will take place. And although these will all happen prior to the Second Coming, still when they do occur, people will know that concluding events are imminent and that the time of Christ's second advent is very near!

In regard to animal sacrifice itself, however, the reintroduction of this ancient practice, will be an extremely unusual and significant occurrence. Certainly it is a concept not always easy to understand, particularly in the context of modern society, and yet it is one that was comprehended fully by Joseph Smith, the man who had so many miraculous experiences during his lifetime and who was the main figure in the process of restitution and restoration.

"The offering of sacrifice," he said on one occasion, "has ever been connected and forms a part of the duties of the Priesthood. It began with the Priesthood and will be continued until after the coming of Christ from generation to generation. We frequently have mention made of the offering of sacrifice by the servants of the Most High in ancient days, prior to the Law of Moses, which ordinances will be continued when the Priesthood is restored with all its authority, power, and blessings."

"These sacrifices, as well as every ordinance belonging to the Priesthood, will when the Temple of the Lord shall be built and the sons of Levi be purified be fully restored and attended to in all their powers, ramifications, and blessings. This ever did and ever will exist when the powers of the Melchizedek Priesthood are sufficiently manifest; else how can the restitution of all things spoken of by the Holy Prophets be brought to pass?"

While it is true that the Law of Moses was fulfilled at the time that Jesus finished his ministry, at which time the Law came to an end, Joseph Smith in his comments on animal sacrifice was quick to point out that the fulfillment and conclusion of the Law itself did not preclude further animal sacrifices sometime in the future. "It is not to be understood," he said, "that the Law of Moses will be established again with all its rites and varieties of ceremonies: this has never been spoken of by the prophets; but those things which existed prior to Moses' day, namely sacrifice, will be continued."[110]

This is also in agreement with something that Jesus himself told the Nephites when he appeared to them on the Western Continent: "And because I said unto you that old things have passed away, I do not destroy that which hath been spoken concerning things which are to come. For behold, the covenant which I have made with my people is not all fulfilled; but the law which was given unto Moses hath an end in me." [111]

One of the main things that Joseph Smith said, therefore, is that animal sacrifice, after it has been restored, will definitely be practiced once again until after the Second Coming of Christ, during which intervening period it will continue "from generation to generation." For whatever reason, this ancient principle will be extended for an indefinite period of time "with all its authority, power, and blessings."

The sacred ordinance which was practiced by Adam and his posterity down through the centuries to the time of Abraham, Isaac, and Jacob, and then to Moses and certain centuries beyond, again will be administered with veneration, not in a symbolic way looking forward to the atonement of Jehovah, but according to a new manner and purpose pertaining to the times of restitution and restoration, all part of the Dispensation of the Fulness of Times.

17

IRONY AND SACRILEGE

The Jewish historian Josephus stated that as many as 256,500 lambs were slain during passover celebrations in Jerusalem, on a single day or possibly two, and also that the actual slaying of the lambs needed to be accomplished between the hours of three and five in the afternoon. This means that if one of the days set apart for this purpose was on the Friday that Jesus was crucified, which is very possible, he died at the same time that the animals themselves began to be killed, it being the ninth hour before his death, or three o'clock.

A terrible irony occurred, therefore, in that the one person whom animal sacrifices down through the centuries actually symbolized, including those being performed in Jerusalem that day, died simultaneously on the cross at the same time that the slaughtering of lambs began in the city below! Hundreds of thousands of people, without knowing what was taking place, prepared to observe the passover.

Josephus gave some idea as to how many people might have been present for the celebrations on that occasion. On the basis of the number of lambs slain for the feast, again estimated to be 256,500, and assuming there would be ten to eleven members at each paschal supper or meal, the calculated number of people involved was 2,700,200, possibly as many as three million or more. This would exclude those in the city who were non-Jewish visitors or those ineligible to participate in the usual celebrations because of ceremonial unfitness.[112]

All of this presents an interesting backdrop to events that occurred on the day that Jesus died. In addition, there were the unique circumstances and conditions in the city itself, a city transformed during the passover into a veritable metropolis in relation to the times.

Of particular significance was the area of the temple where Jesus had taught on many occasions and also a nearby area where the mass sacrifice of animals would take place. The temple area itself, for example, was undoubtedly a noticeable center of activity, as well as confusion. The designated stations close by where the paschal lambs were killed must have presented an almost unbelievable spectacle in comparison with a modern religious celebration. Many things were occurring in these two places at the time that Jesus was being prepared for execution and taken to the hill known as Calvary or Golgotha.

The large area immediately south of the temple was called the Court of the Gentiles, and it was here during the ministry of Jesus that people had become accustomed to bringing in large numbers of oxen and sheep, as well as doves, and putting them on sale for sacrifices. Pens and wicker cages were everywhere, and the stench and filth caused by a large number of animals and birds, along with the noise they made, were repulsive and interfered with what was meant to be a place of reverence and sanctity.

In addition to the inevitable bartering and bargaining which took place, there were also the money-changers pursuing their trade, all of which must have contrasted with the activity of Levites and priests nearby who were closer to the temple proper.

Certainly the temple had become not only a place of commerce, taking on the appearance of an auction or country fair, but also a place of sacrilege. It is no wonder that Jesus at the beginning of his ministry became angry at the people and "drove them all out of the temple, and the sheep, and the oxen, and poured out the changers' money, and overthrew the tables."[113]

But it was at the different places of animal sacrifice, where thousands of lambs were about to be killed, that the real sacrilege, as well as irony, took place. At exactly three o'clock on Friday afternoon, at about the same time that Jesus died, the traditional sacrificing of animals for the passover began. After centuries of ceremonial observance in which mankind paid allegiance to Deity for whatever purpose, whether in similitude of the infinite sacrifice of Jehovah or in reverence to some unknown god, the real purpose intended was finally fulfilled and consummated. The ancient principle of sacrifice, the validity of which was terminated until a time of latter-day restitution, was ended in Jerusalem that day when the Lord himself said, "It is finished," and then bowed his head and yielded up the ghost.

18

THE SEVENTH MILLENNIUM

According to scripture, no one knows when the Second Coming will be except one person, and that is God the Father. "But of that day and hour knoweth no man," Jesus said, "no, not the angels in heaven, but my Father only."[114]

Because the Father and the Son are one in mind and purpose, however, totally in one accord concerning all things, it might be that Jesus excluded himself in making this statement. But the scripture says otherwise, and either way it emphasizes the idea of secrecy and the importance of being prepared.

Various predictions have been made in the past concerning the end of the world and the time of Christ's Second Coming. Sometimes exact dates have been given and even specific times of arrival. Also at the beginning of the year 2000, and during the year that followed, there were those who viewed the calendar with increased interest and wondered if something highly significant might take place, something connected with the turning of a century and the start of a new millennium.

All of this was speculation, of course, and came from a large number of sources and viewpoints. It reflected many different kinds of beliefs, one of them being a certain concept attributed to Joseph Smith which he said he received by revelation in 1832 and recorded in a book entitled The Doctrine and Covenants. The concept referred specifically to the Second Coming of Jesus Christ but gave no exact date as to when it would be. It said only that the event would occur sometime in the beginning of the seventh millennium.

The millennium in question, Joseph explained, was the seventh thousand years since the time of Adam and Eve in the Garden of Eden. It was to be the final millennium in the earth's normal history, the last of "the seven thousand years of its continuance, or its temporal existence."

"We are to understand," according to the revelation, "that as God made the world in six says, and on the seventh day he finished his work and sanctified it, and also formed man out of the dust of the earth, even so, in the beginning of the seventh thousand years will the Lord God sanctify the earth and complete the salvation of man, and judge all things and shall redeem all things except that which he hath not put into his power, when he shall have sealed all things unto the end of all things.

"And the sounding of the trumpets of the seven angels," referring to the opening of the seventh seal spoken of in the Book of Revelation, "is the preparing and finishing of his work in the beginning of the seventh thousand years—the preparing of the way before the time of his coming."[115]

In very few places in modern scripture is there so much information given in such a small number of words. The import of its content is almost beyond description. Again this was not material composed by Joseph Smith himself, but information which he claimed to have received through revelation and later recorded in The Doctrine and Covenants.

The confirmation that six thousand years of world history have taken place so far is in itself a remarkable statement. But what is more significant is that sometime in the beginning of the seventh millennium, however long that beginning period might be, the one in charge of the earth's destiny, even Jehovah, will begin the process of finishing his work, "the preparing of the way before the time of his coming."

The Second Coming, therefore, according to this scripture, will likely occur sometime during the present century, although too much is yet to happen for the event to take place in just a matter of years, or even possibly within a few decades. Indeed, reference to the beginning of a millennium could mean as much as a century or more, one tenth of a thousand years or at least the major part of it. Ancient and modern scripture both require it, dictating that in connection with religious prophecy, certain things definitely need to occur as part of a final preparation.

One of the first things that must occur is related to temple building. Prophecy and scripture both state that prior to the Second Coming a major temple is to be constructed not only in America but in Palestine as well. These will not be just ordinary temples, but edifices characteristic of a city of Zion, such as one that might have existed in the days of Enoch. They will be sacred structures representative of two world capitals, one located in the central part of the United States and the other in the city of Jerusalem in the Eastern Hemisphere.

Any serious indication or advance notice pertaining to the Second Coming will undoubtedly depend upon the building of these two temples. Among those who are aware of the history involved, and also religious prophecies, they will be a major sign of the times. Certainly when the construction of these buildings is commenced, people will then know that the time of the Lord's Second Advent is definitely near, even imminent, although possibly still generations away.

Other preliminary events, all having major significance, will be (1) an important religious conference scheduled to occur at a place called Adam-ondi-Ahman, (2) a mammoth earthquake beyond anything previously known, (3) highly unusual astronomic phenomena pertaining to the sun, moon, and stars, (4) the widespread occurrence of plagues and pestilence, and (5) the catastrophic Battle of Armageddon. In addition there will be (6) the spectacular return of the lost Ten Tribes from the north country, said by some to be prior to the Second Coming, by others following the beginning of the Millennium.

Finally, in this same general time period, conditions on the earth itself will be drastically altered and changed. The waters of the great deep, spoken of in both ancient and modern scripture and presumably referring mainly to the Atlantic and Pacific Oceans, will recede in a northerly direction, causing vast land changes. This will take place at the command of Jehovah, who at some time will make a dramatic appearance on the Mount of Olives in Jerusalem at the conclusion of the Battle of Armageddon.

"He shall command the great deep, and it shall be driven back into the north countries, and the islands shall become one land; and the land of Jerusalem and the land of Zion shall be turned back into their own place, and the earth shall be like as it was in the days before it was divided. And the Lord, even the Savior, shall stand in the midst of his people and shall reign over all flesh."[116]

Once again most of these events might still be relatively distant, although even at the doors as far as a scriptural viewpoint is concerned. But they nonetheless need to be accomplished and will be part of the preparing and finishing of the Lord's work and "the preparing of the way before the time of his coming." And one of the events will necessarily be the building of an American temple in Zion.

The restoration of animal sacrifice will also occur before the Second Coming. This will be part of the restitution of all things as well as an important link with principles and ordinances of the past, it will be an additional sign of the times, indicating that something highly significant is about to take place. The resumption of a principle that people have generally regarded as being concluded and fulfilled at the time of the Atonement, never to be practiced again except briefly and symbolically, will once more be a signal that the Savior's Second Advent is drawing near.

Surely this will be a unique time in history, and in some ways a perplexing one since the question definitely exists as to why such an ancient ordinance as animal sacrifice again needs to be observed. And as to a possible answer, the only known reason is one stated very briefly by Joseph Smith in a general church conference held in 1840.

He said, "It may be asked by some what necessity for sacrifice, since the Great Sacrifice was offered. In answer to which, if repentance, baptism, and faith existed prior to the time of Christ, what necessity for them since that time?"[117] Again his answer was very brief, and people might speculate as to what Joseph actually meant, but the idea that this type of sacrifice would someday be resumed was nevertheless clearly stated.

Certainly words cannot adequately describe the magnitude and significance of events leading up to the Second Coming of Jesus Christ. Such events will not only herald and accompany a second advent but will provide a grand panorama of miraculous occurrences in recognition of a returning King. Everything that has been predicted in ancient and modern prophesy will be fulfilled. No aspect of preparation will be left undone. And in the process, after six thousand years of world history has come to an end and a seventh one begun, Jehovah will again carry out the will of his Father by introducing a new era of human affairs, including the emergence of a paradisiacal earth and the time predicted by prophets of old known as the Millennium.

19

A LIST OF NAMES

When Jesus was sent to earth to prepare for an earthly ministry, he carried with him important skills and information, attributes which would come to fruition as he grew older and "increased in wisdom and stature." These included (1) an inherent power over life and death, (2) complete control of the forces of nature, (3) knowledge of how to heal the sick, cast out devils, and raise the dead, (4) authority to preach the gospel to the lost sheep of the House of Israel, and (5) knowledge of how to perform the infinite atonement and implement the resurrection.

All of these things he received specifically from his Father. In addition, he had a list of names identifying people who were qualified and capable of receiving his message and consequently would believe in him as the Messiah.

The individuals on this list, according to the fore-knowledge of God, were those that would readily accept the gospel, people who had been tried and tested in premortal life and who had remained faithful during their second estate in mortality. They were the ones who were obedient and dependable in their allegiance to the Father and the Son. Jesus referred to them once as his sheep and said specifically that they had been given to him by his Father.

"My sheep hear my voice, and I know them," he said, "and they follow me: and I give unto them eternal life; and they shall never perish, neither shall any man pluck them out of my hand. My Father, which gave them me, is greater than all; and no man is able to pluck them out of my Father's hand."[118]

The word "pluck" is often used in the Bible, but only in this one instance is it used in connection with people recognized by both the Father and the Son as being true and faithful and who merit eternal life. Again they were those on the list, as it were, a symbolic list that Jesus brought with him when he came from his Father's presence.

It is interesting to view the people in Palestine at this time within this particular context. Definitely there were those individuals who were the ones Jesus recognized as his sheep, those who had actually been given to him beforehand. Because of righteousness and good works during premortal life, they were foreordained to be among those most valiant on earth in respecting Deity and carrying out Heaven's plan. This is not to say that they were destined or predetermined to do so in violation of their agency, but according to the foreknowledge of the Father, he knew how they would react during their stay on earth and consequently gave them to his Son as candidates for eternal life.

"All that the Father giveth me shall come to me," Jesus said, "and him that cometh to me I will in no wise cast out. And this is the Father's will which hath sent me, that of all which he hath given me I should lose nothing, but will raise it up again at the last day."[119]

This group of people was undoubtedly discussed and determined jointly by Jehovah and his Father before the foundation of the earth. During the Son's ministry the Father took a special interest in their affairs.. He is the one, for example, who possessed righteous people in the beginning, or regarded them as his own, and who in turn gave them to his Son who through his atoning sacrifice would raise them up at the last day.

It must have been disappointing to Jesus, however, when he saw the majority of people rejecting him. On the day that he delivered the "Bread of Life" sermon in the synagogue in Capernaum, at a time when "many of his disciples went back and walked no more with him," he even questioned his own apostles, asking if they too were thinking of going away. Yet again he knew in advance, as did his Father, who it was that would believe or not believe his message.[120]

But it was actually on the occasion of the Last Supper, attended by Jesus and the twelve apostles, when it became most evident that God himself had determined that certain people were at a level of right-eousness entitling them to be the personal property, as it were, of Deity. During the great intercessory prayer which Jesus offered at that time, he prayed not for the world in general but specifically for the men who had followed him in his ministry.

"I have manifested thy name unto the men which thou gavest me out of the world," he said, speaking to his Father. "Thine they were, and thou gavest them me; and they have kept thy word . . . I pray for them: I pray not for the world, but for them which thou hast given me; for they are thine. And all mine are thine, and thine are mine; and I am glorified in them.

"While I was with them in the world, I kept them in thy name: those that thou gavest me I have kept, and none of them is lost, but the son of perdition; that the scripture might be fulfilled . . . And now I am no more in the world," Jesus concluded, " but these are in the world, and I come to thee. Holy Father, keep through thine own name those whom thou hast given me, that they may be one, as we are."[121]

It was the Father, therefore, who was overseer to all that was transpiring on earth. He was the one during the Son's ministry who positioned people at designated times and places where, according to their agency and inclination, they could promote heaven's plan or obstruct it. At this strategic time in history, He gave people the opportunity either to accept the Son or reject him, while at the same time knowing who had prepared themselves for this particular moment. "Every plant which my heavenly Father hath not planted shall be rooted up," Jesus said.[122] And as a result of all this, the harvesting as well as the planting, along with the presence of a divine ministry, people on earth acted out their parts, and the eternal consequences were always there.

20

THE BITTER CUP

None of the things that Jehovah took with him to earth as part of his mission was more important than a certain cup which he referred to on several different occasions. Although a cup with one meaning or another is mentioned several times in scripture, the cup that Jesus now possessed was one specifically given to him by his Father. He alluded to it once while speaking to Peter who was trying to protect him from bodily injury.

"The cup which my Father hath given me," he said while restraining Peter, "shall I not drink it?"[123]

This particular cup, although metaphorical in meaning, was one of the things which Jehovah received and carried with him upon leaving the presence of his Father. It was part of the light and knowledge, as well as the specific assignment, that had been given to him.

There was also a cup in a different sense which he had used earlier as described by the Psalmist: "For in the hand of the Lord there is a cup," the scripture states, "and the wine is red; it is full of mixture; and he poureth out the same; but the dregs thereof, all the wicked of the earth shall wring them out, and drink them. But I will declare forever; I will sing praises to the God of Jacob."[124]

The God of Jacob, of course, was Jehovah, and the red wine which he poured from the cup was rich in mixture. But aside from the symbolism intended in the scripture, the cup that Jesus possessed throughout his ministry was not only symbolic and metaphorical, but in another sense very real. Again it was something he brought with him from his Father, and he referred to it several times, especially as the time drew near for his atonement and crucifixion.

As to the contents of the cup, some indication of what they were was given in an incident one day when the apostles James and John, along with their mother, came to Jesus and made an important request. At that time, they asked that in the Kingdom of Heaven in the future the two men might have seats of honor beside the Lord, one on his right hand and the other on the left. This displeased the other apostles, but to James and John, and especially the mother, it nevertheless seemed important enough to ask for such a favor.

It was then that Jesus spoke not only of drinking from the cup, but also of being baptized, not with a baptism of water but one of blood and death. The latter was in reference to the persecution that he must suffer, along with his eventual crucifixion.

"Are ye able to drink of the cup that I shall drink of," he asked, "and to be baptized with the baptism that I am baptized with?"[125]

The apostles answered that they were ready, and as things turned out, they were right, because both of them proved willing to do all that Jesus did and to sacrifice their lives if necessary for the sake of the gospel. But at the same time, they were also very much unaware of what was in store for them, unlike Jesus, who knew only too well what was ahead.

In the cup, therefore, which Jesus possessed, was an assignment and commission given by the Father to preform a mission on earth and carry out an infinite atonement in behalf of mankind. It was an assignment that had been preceded earlier by a foreordination before the foundation of the world, followed by the calling and election to be the Messiah and Savior of mankind. It also contained an implication of the tremendous responsibilities involved, as well as inevitable persecution and death.

Thus at a very early time period, Jehovah was foreordained to be not just the Messiah, but specifically "the Lamb slain from the foundation of the world."[126] There would not only be rejection and oppression but eventual death by execution. All of this he knew by way of the cup that had been given to him by his Father.

Undoubtedly, Jesus was aware of certain details, yet apparently unaware also of how everything would exactly transpire. But one thing he did know, and that was that he must die in order for an atonement to occur. "Except a corn of wheat fall into the ground and die," he once told Philip and Andrew, "it abideth alone: but if it die, it bringeth forth much fruit."

At this time he also admitted that his soul was troubled, speaking to the apostles personally or contemplating within himself. The question was whether or not to ask the Father if there was any possible way he might be spared from at least some of the things that lay ahead.

"Father, save me from this hour," he must have thought. And then he said quickly, "But for this cause came I unto this hour." He knew that ultimately everything would be according to his Father's will, yet he knew also that with God all things were possible.

For a long time Jesus had known that an ignominious death was imminent and would in some way be related to the cross. Soon after talking to the apostles, for example, he turned and spoke to some people nearby. "Now is the judgment of this world," he told them. "Now shall the prince of this world be cast out. And I, if I be lifted up from the earth, will draw all men unto me."[127]

Once again there was the implication that he would not be acting in and of himself but would be carrying out the will of his Father. These same ideas were expressed in modern scripture: "And my Father sent me that I might be lifted upon the cross, and after that I had been lifted up upon the cross, that I might draw all men unto me, that as I have been lifted up by men even so should men be lifted up by the Father, to stand before me, to be judged of their works, whether they be good or whether they be evil. And for this cause have I been lifted up."[128]

Certainly it had been prophesied that Jesus would be crucified and his body laid in a sepulcher, also that before his death he would be subjected to all manner of persecution. But the details of everything would never exactly be known until they had actually taken place, and whatever it was that happened would be up to the will and choosing of the Father.

During his growing up years, Jesus must have often remembered the story of Abraham and his son Isaac, and how the story turned out on that occasion, and what words the Lord used when he called to Abraham and said there was an alternative way to conduct the sacrifice. Now on the eve of his own coming sacrifice, he undoubtedly knew that it had been he himself who called to Abraham that day and said, "Lay not thine hand upon the lad, neither do thou anything unto him."[129]

Moreover, he possibly had this same kind of remembrance at later time in the Garden of Gethsemane when he commenced the long and tedious process of the atonement. It was there that he again approached his Father, not only in thought, but in verbal prayer, and asked once more if there was any way he could avoid some of the things which were ahead of him, possibly not only in the garden but between there and the cross as well.

Previously he had emphasized that with God all things were possible[130], and now with his own personal status and welfare at stake, as it had been with Isaac on that day in the land of Moriah, he importuned his Father three different times for possible relief in the Garden of Gethsemane.

"Abba, Father," he said at the first, "all things are possible unto thee; take away this cup from me; nevertheless not what I will, but what thou wilt." Then later during a second time, and according to a different account, he prayed a little differently by saying, "Oh my Father, if this cup may not pass away from me, except I drink it, thy will be done."[131] And on still a third time, he said basically the same things before finally retiring with Judas Iscariot and those who had come to arrest him.

In that lonely garden, therefore, in the place where Jesus had spent so many hours with the twelve apostles, he again repeated the words that had become his trade mark, as it were, those which left an expression of his own will up to the discretion of his Father. And as he himself had once made the decision to spare Isaac, providing another solution or alternate way, he now suggested a similar possibility in regard to his own Father, not knowing for certain what the final decision would be.

As to the outcome, however, it all came down to the assignment that Jesus had from the beginning, that which was in the cup that he had brought from his Father. Such a cup contained all of the information and instruction necessary concerning that part of the Lord's mission which pertained to the atonement. In a symbolic yet very realistic way, it outlined what it was he needed to do, and eventually had to do.

And as to the cup being specifically a bitter cup, reference to such is found in modern scripture, on the occasion when Jesus visited the people known as the Nephites sometime following his death and resurrection and his ascension into heaven. "Behold, I am Jesus Christ," he told them at that time, "whom the prophets testified should come into the world.

"And behold, I am the light and the life of the world; and I have drunk out of that bitter cup which the Father hath given me, and have glorified the Father in taking upon me the sins of the world, in the which I have suffered the will of the Father in all things from the beginning.

"Arise and come forth unto me," he said, "that ye

may thrust your hands into my side, and also that ye may feel the prints of the nails in my hands and in my feet, that ye may know that I am the God of Israel, and the God of the whole earth, and have been slain for the sins of the world!"[132]

21

A HEAVENLY VISION

While Adam and Eve were in the Garden of Eden, at the very beginning of human history, it was the Father who corresponded with them and gave them instructions. Following the Fall, however, after they had eaten the forbidden fruit, Jehovah assumed the administration of human affairs, and it was he who spoke to mankind from that time forward, revealing himself mainly by way of the prophets.

This means that it was Jehovah who spoke not only to Adam but also to Enoch, the latter being taken into heaven and an entire city with him. Later the Savior walked and talked with Noah, telling him that the people's destruction was imminent because of their wickedness and that a gigantic flood was about to come upon the earth.

Then, through the different time periods, Jehovah communed with Abraham, Isaac, and Jacob, and eventually with Moses who received instructions to lead the Lord's people out of Egyptian bondage. Especially on this latter occasion did it become more apparent who the God of Israel was, and that it was he who was guiding the affairs of mankind.

It was Jehovah, in other words, who spoke to

Moses out of the burning bush and gave him the Ten Commandments on tables of stone on Mount Sinai. He was the one who talked with him in the tabernacle of the congregation, "face to face, as a man speaketh unto his friend."[133]

After that time, the Lord continued to speak through his servants the prophets, giving commandments and instructions and detailing what it was that needed to be done. Noteworthy especially were the instances in the Old Testament when Jehovah spoke to Isaiah, Jeremiah, and Ezekiel.

But eventually, sometime after the time of the prophet Malachi, there was a spiritual famine in the land. The House of Israel, which had been divided and dispersed among the nations, no longer existed as a political institution, and during the centuries immediately preceding the birth of Jesus and his ministry upon the earth, the entire world, including the Jews themselves, was in a state of religious depression and apostasy.

Even while Jesus was personally among the people, it was not much different. Most of those whom he taught were belligerent or disbelieving. And after Christianity was established as a religion, there were also the difficult years when the church he had organized began to change from its original structure and doctrine. One by one, most of the apostles were killed, after which a long period of history began that included a continuing apostasy and the centuries of dark ages, followed by the times of reformation and enlightenment.

But then finally came the time in the beginning of

the 19th century when the man known as Joseph Smith made his appearance in modern history. It was he who said he had received a vision, not an uncommon thing historically but one that was unique in that he spoke of two people appearing to him and announcing themselves as the Father and the Son! Never before had anyone made this kind of statement, and it resulted in a completely new doctrine of Deity that was eventually publicized throughout the world.

One of the theories pertaining to Christianity up to that point had been that Jesus and his Father were not separate persons, but were part of a Holy Trinity including the Holy Ghost. The Trinity consists of three personages or identities yet in some way were regarded as one individual. But the vision which Joseph Smith received definitely involved two people, standing above him in the air according to his description, one referring to himself as the Father and acknowledging the other as his Son.

Joseph's experience at that time was in response to a prayer which he offered in a grove of trees not far from his home. His purpose was an ordinary one, such as that of anyone earnestly seeking for truth, yet he was undoubtedly very surprised at the kind of answer he received. What he did not know, however, was that he had been set apart much earlier, foreordained and elected to do exactly what he was doing!

"After I had retired to the place where I had previously designed to go," he said, "having looked around me and finding myself alone, I kneeled down and began to offer up the desire of my heart to God." According to his own account, this was a new experience for him, since he had never before made the attempt to pray vocally.

At the first, there was a type of opposition or resistance, which he later described in detail, and when it was over, he experienced a remarkable vision. "I saw a pillar of light exactly over my head," he recalled, "above the brightness of the sun, which descended gradually until it fell upon me." "When the light rested upon me, I saw two personages, whose brightness and glory defy all description, standing above me in the air. One of them spake unto me, calling me by name, and said pointing to the other—"This is my beloved Son. Hear him!"

Again the details of the vision were not given until a subsequent time, but the main thing that Joseph Smith learned that day was that God the Father and his Son were not two persons incorporated into one, but instead were two separate individuals with corporeal bodies of flesh and bones, two resurrected personages who had appeared on earth and condescended to speak to a man.

Like Philip in the New Testament, Joseph had probably wondered what the Father was like in relation to the Son. Were they two separate people, for example, or two spiritual identities combined in one? "Show us the Father," Philip had said, "and it sufficeth us." The answer Jesus gave at that time was not entirely clear, and it continued to puzzle people for centuries as they attempted to read and interpret the scriptures.

"He that hath seen me hath seen the Father," Jesus told Philip, meaning that in likeness and appearance, the two were basically the same. Still there were questions, however, people being subject to a variety of opinions and never really knowing for certain about the true nature of God.

Yet what took place in the grove that day not only answered the specific questions of Joseph Smith, but it answered once and for all the question pertaining to a true concept of Deity. The Father and the Son were definitely two separate individuals, in other words, the one being the supreme authority and the other in charge of all human affairs acting in the Father's behalf. Certainly an entirely new dimension pertaining to the Godhead was at that time introduced into religion.

And unlike Thomas, another of the early apostles, who was not convinced of something until he had seen things for himself, those who believed in Joseph's report of the heavenly vision now became part of a very exclusive group, viewing Deity from a very new perspective. Indeed they became part of a grand process of restitution and restoration. Whereas people might have been uncertain as to what God was really like, they now had an entirely different concept in which to place their faith, one that involved two separate glorified beings, each with a resurrected body of flesh and bones and together presiding over the affairs of the universe as the Father and the Son.

Note

Today among much of the world population, Jesus is accepted as a great man or prophet but not as a God. The Father, or someone comparable to him, is regarded as God, often a spirit or force in the universe, but not necessarily anything similar to a man.

The principle and doctrine of Deity introduced by Joseph Smith, however, definitely states that God is a glorified resurrected man with a corporeal body, and likewise the Son who is a separate individual in the express image and likeness of his Father.

References

Note: The King James version of the Bible, The Book of Mormon, The Doctrine and Covenants, and The Pearl of Great Price are standard works of The Church of Jesus Christ of Latter-day Saints.

1. Doctrine and Covenants 93:30.
2. Doctrine and Covenants 93:31-32.
3. Romans 8:29.
4. Doctrine and Covenants 93:30.
5. Helaman 14:30.
6. 2 Nephi 2:26.
7. Alma 12:31.
8. Doctrine and Covenants 93:31-32.
9. Gordon Allred (Comp.), *God the Father* (Salt Lake City: Deseret News Company, 1979), p. 185.
10. Ibid.
11. Joseph Smith, *History of the Church of Jesus Christ of Latter-Day Saints* (Salt Lake City: Deseret Book Company, 1950), Vol. 6, p. 305.
12. Gordon Allred (Comp.), *God the Father* (Salt Lake City: Deseret News Company, 1979), p. 192.
13. Ibid., p. 185.
14. Abraham 3:2-4.
15. Romans 8:29.
16. Psalms 89:27-28.
17. Colossians 1:15.
18. Revelation 3:14.
19. Doctrine and Covenants 93:31-32.
20. Acts 17:28-29.
21. Doctrine and Covenants 76:24.
22. Abraham 3:24-26.
23. Ibid., 3:27-28.
24. Revelation 12:4, 7-8.

25. Ibid., 12:9.

26. Genesis 1:1-2.

27. John 1:3, 10.

28. Romans 8:29.

29. Doctrine and Covenants 76:24.

30. Abraham 4:1, 3-4.

31. Romans 8:30.

32. Abraham 3:22-23.

33. Deuteronomy 32:7-8.

34. Genesis 35:10.

35. Acts 17:26.

36. Deuteronomy 32:8.

37. Exodus 6:3.

38. Psalms 93:18.

39. 3 Nephi 15:5, 9.

40. Ibid., 9:15, 10:4-5.

41. Isaiah 29:14; Ephesians 1:9-10.

42. Joseph Smith, *History of the Church of Jesus Christ of Latter-day Saints* (Salt Lake City: Deseret Book Company, 1951), Vol. 1, p. 5.

43. Amos 9:9.

44. John 10:16.

45. 3 Nephi 15:21, 24.

46. Ibid., 9:12.

47. Ibid., 16:1-3.

48. Bruce M. Metzger (Ed.), *The Apocrypha of the Old Testament*, Revised Standard Version (New York: Oxford University Press, 1965), p. 65 (2 Esdras 13:41-45).

49. Doctrine and Covenants 133:26-27.

50. Metzger, op. cit., p. 65.

51. Doctrine and Covenants 133:26-27.

52. 3 Nephi 17:4.

53. Metzger, op. cit., p. 65.

54. Doctrine and Covenants 133:26.

55. R. Clayton Brough, *The Lost Tribes* (Salt Lake City: Horizon Publishers, 1979), p. 44.

56. 3 Nephi 15:13-15.

57. H.R. Hall, *The Ancient History of the Near East* (London: Methuen and Company, 1913). p. 466. Others have since expressed this same view, pointing out that only a part of a conquered area was taken abroad into captivity.

58. Matthew 15:24.

59. Doctrine and Covenants 133:32-33.

60. Moses 1:32-33, 37-38.

61. Doctrine and Covenants 76:22-24.

62. 3 Nephi 17:4.

63. Ibid. 24:1.

64. Ibid. 25:4.

65. John 12:49-50.

66. Moses 4:2.

67. Jeremiah 1:5.

68. Romans 8:29-30.

69. Ibid., 9:6.

70. Ibid., 9:7-8.

71. Abraham 1:16.

72. Ibid., 2:11.

73. Genesis 12:2-3.

74. Doctrine and Covenants 105:35.

75. Matthew 20:16.

76. Luke 2:52.

77. Genesis 22:14.

78. Matthew 3:16-17.

79. Mark 9:7; John 12:28.

80. Mark 1:13.

81. John 5:30.

82. Ibid., 8:19.

83. Ibid., 14:7-9.

84. Genesis 5:3.

85. Doctrine and Covenants 107:43.

86. John 12:44-45.

87. Ibid., 10:30.

88. Ibid., 17-22.

89. Genesis 1:26.

90. Joseph Smith, *History of the Church of Jesus Christ of Latter-day Saints* (Salt Lake City: Deseret Book Company, 1951), Vol. 1, p. 5.

91. Matthew 10:40.

92. John 1:1-2.

93. Ibid., Revised Version.

94. Luke 4:43.

95. Matthew 15:24.

96. Hebrews 3:1.

97. John 12:44.

98. Ibid., 5:23.

99. Matthew 10:33.

100. Luke 10:16.

101. John 17:3.

102. Ibid., 5:19-20.

103. Ibid., 5:21.

104. Ibid., 10:17-18.

105. Ibid., 5:19.

106. Joseph Smith, *History of the Church of Jesus Christ of Latter-day Saints* (Sat Lake City: Deseret Book Company, 1950), Vol. 6, pp. 305-306.

107. Flavius Josephus, *Complete Works of Flavius Josephus* (Grand Rapids: Kregel Publications, 1960), *The Wars of the Jews,* Book 2, Chapter 14, #3; Book 6, Chapter 9, #3.

108. 3 Nephi 9:19-20.

109. Acts 3:21; Ephesians 1:10.

110. Joseph Smith, *History of the Church of Jesus Christ of Latter-day Saints* (Salt Lake City: Deseret Book Company, 1949), Vol. 4, pp. 211-212.

111. 3 Nephi 15:7-8.

112. Flavius Josephus, *Complete Works of Flavius Josephus* (Grand Rapids: Kregel Publications, 1960), *The Wars of the Jews,* Book 2, Chapter 14, #3; Book 6, Chapter 9, #3.

113. John 2:15.

114. Matthew 24:36.

115. Doctrine and Covenants 77:12.

116. Ibid., 133:23-25.

117. Joseph Smith, *History of the Church of Jesus Christ of Latter- day Saints* (Salt Lake City: Deseret Book Company, 1949), Vol. 4, p. 212.

118. John 10:27-29.

119. Ibid., 6:37, 39.

120. Ibid., 6:64.

121. Ibid., 17:6, 9-12.

122. Matthew 15:13.

123. John 18:11.

124. Psalms 75:8.

125. Matthew 20:22.

126. Revelation 13:8.

127. John 12:24, 27, 31-32.

128. 3 Nephi 27:14-15.

129. Genesis 22:12.

130. Mark 10:27.

131. Mark 14:36; Matthew 26:42.

132. 3 Nephi 11;10-11, 14.

About the Author

Clay McConkie is a native of Utah. He is a teacher by occupation, having taught in the Salt Lake City Schools for thirty years. He received a B.A. from Brigham Young University and an M.S. and Ph.D. from the University of Utah. He and his wife reside in Provo, Utah, and are the parents of four children.

He is also the author of *One Flesh, The Gathering of the Waters, The Ten Lost Tribes*, and *A Man Named Peleg*.

9 26575 77751 5